MILES DAVIS

FOR BEGINNERS

DARYL N. LONG *Writers and Readers*

WRITERS AND READERS PUBLISHING, INCORPORATED
P.O. Box 461, Village Station
New York, NY 10014

c/o Airlift Book Company
26 Eden Grove
London N7 8EF
England

A Writers and Readers Documentary Comic Book
Copyright © 1992
Library of Congress Catalog Card Number 92-050415
ISBN # 0-86316-154-5 Cloth
ISBN # 0-86316-153-7 Trade
1 2 3 4 5 6 7 8 9 0

Manufactured in the United States of America

this book is dedicated to my Mother for all that
she's had to endure.
to Chris, Austin & DeShawn. Carry on.
to Karen & Kathy.
to Dad, Mama Della, & Aunt Addie,
& a mi Olacita.

In all
of jazz
so far, Miles's horn is
perhaps the most subtle
delineator of loneliness. A
prideful loneliness, to be sure, but
no less a chronic condition for
all of that. He is, of course, never
sentimental,
however introspective. Instead, he tends to be, as a
French musician once said to me, "insidious, like
somebody calling you from the other shore."
- Nat Hentoff, *Jazz Is*

IT WINDS AROUND JAZZ CIRCLES, SO YOU MAY
HAVE HEARD IT BEFORE. ITS SOURCE IS UNCLEAR —
PERHAPS A HIPSTER SEANCE. SIX RETRO-BOP JAZZMEN
IN A CIRCLE. DRESSED. CLEANER THAN BROKE-DICK
DOGS. LOOKING TO MAKE CONTACT WITH THE
ANCESTORS. HOPING TO PICK UP ON THEIR
VIBE BEFORE THE NEXT SET.

IT'S TOLD THAT UPON HIS PASSING, THE GREAT
JAZZ BASSIST, **CHARLIE MINGUS**, WAS WANDERING
AROUND HEAVEN WHEN HE RAN INTO THE LEGENDARY
TENOR AND SOPRANO SAX MAN, **JOHN COLTRANE**.
WHILE TRANE WAS GIVING MINGUS THE GRAND TOUR
THEY CAME UPON THIS *BIG CAT*, WITH A LONG WHITE
BEARD, ROCKING IN THE CHAIR-OF-AGES. MINGUS IS
SAID TO HAVE ASKED, "SAY JIM, (JAZZMEN CALL
EVERYBODY 'JIM') *WHO THE HELL IS THAT?*" COLTRANE
SHOOK HIS HEAD AND FROWNED, "*I DON'T KNOW, BUT HE
THINKS HE'S MILES.*"

TO SOME NOTHING ELSE NEED BE WRITTEN. TO OTHERS,
THE JAZZ GODHEAD IS A TRINITY COMPRISING **LOUIE
ARMSTRONG, DUKE ELLINGTON** AND **CHARLIE
"YARDBIRD" PARKER**, BETTER KNOWN AS "**BIRD**."

Blue Note

"Cleaner than a broke-dick dog" is a phrase Miles picked up as a kid growing up in St. Louis. Although we could speculate as to its origin, we won't do so here. Let it suffice to say that it means that you're well-groomed and dressed in some pretty hip threads.

5

REGARDLESS OF WHOSE ALTAR YOU CHOOSE TO
KNEEL BEFORE, ONE THING IS CLEAR: MORE THAN
ANY OTHER PLAYER, MILES DAVIS HAS PUSHED
JAZZ IN NEW DIRECTIONS, DEFINED AND REFINED
NEW ELEMENTS AND SOUNDS, AND EXPLORED
AND EXPLOITED NEW IDEAS AND TECHNOLOGIES.
FROM *BEBOP* TO *DOO-BOP*, MILES STOOD AT THE
EDGE, POISED, HORN DOWN, ELBOWS AT HIS SIDE,
BACK TO THE CROWD, MOODILY BREATHING NEW
LIFE INTO THE MUSIC.

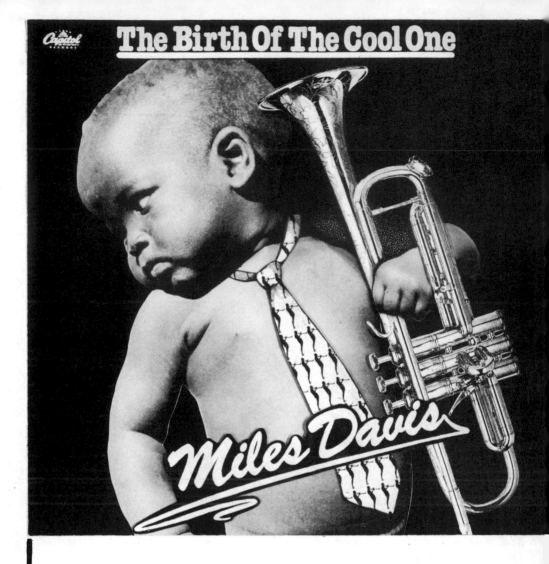

Miles Davis

MILES DEWEY DAVIS III WAS BORN IN ALTON, ILLINOIS, ON MAY 25, 1926, TO MILES AND CLEOTA DAVIS. EVERYONE CALLED HIM JUNIOR.

"I ALWAYS HATED THAT NICKNAME."

THE DAVIS FAMILY MOVED TO EAST ST. LOUIS SHORTLY AFTER JUNIOR'S BIRTH.

LIKE DUKE ELLINGTON, MILES WAS BORN INTO AN AFFLUENT AFRICAN-AMERICAN HOME. HIS GRANDFATHER WAS AN EXPERT BOOKKEEPER WHO EARNED A GOOD DEAL OF MONEY FROM HIS WHITE NEIGHBORS IN ARKANSAS — AS MUCH AS $100 A DAY DURING THE GREAT DEPRESSION. (UNFORTUNATELY, THE IDEA OF A BLACK MAN GETTING RICH OFF A WHITE MAN'S GREEN, DIDN'T SIT WELL WITH HIS CLIENTELE.) SO ALONG WITH THEIR MONEY, HE EARNED THEIR ENDURING ANIMOSITY. MILES'S FATHER, REFERRED TO AS DOC DAVIS, WAS A DENTIST WITH *HIS* FATHER'S HEAD FOR BUSINESS. HE WAS BLESSED WITH HIS FATHER'S FLAIR FOR SUCCESS AS WELL.

BUT WAIT.

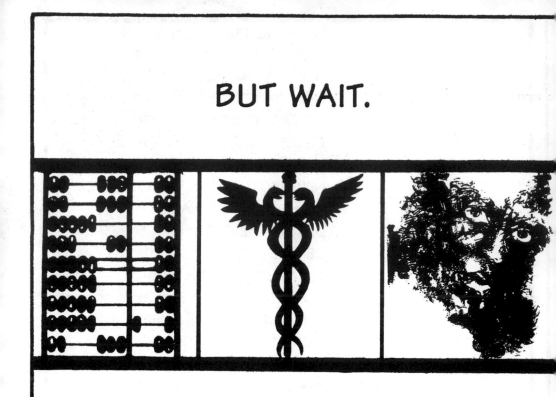

BOOKKEEPER? DENTIST? RECLUSIVE, ENIGMATIC TRUMPET PLAYER CALLED THE COOL ONE, THE BLACK PRINCE, THE MAN WITH THE HORN?

WHAT'S WRONG WITH THIS PICTURE?

NOTHING REALLY. IN AN INTERVIEW WITH WRITER MARC CRAWFORD IN 1961, MILES'S FATHER EXPLAINED IT THIS WAY: *"HISTORICALLY WAY BACK INTO SLAVERY DAYS, THE DAVISES HAVE BEEN MUSICIANS AND PERFORMED CLASSIC WORKS IN THE HOMES OF THE PLANTATION OWNERS."*

MUSIC, HOWEVER, WAS NOT JUNIOR'S ONLY LOVE. BUT, FORTUNATELY FOR US HE WAS A LITTLE TOO SKINNY IN THE LEGS TO BE A CHAMPION PRIZEFIGHTER OR A JIM BROWN TYPE MOTHERFUCKER♪ ON THE GRIDIRON. DOC AND CLEOTA DAVIS, HOWEVER, HAD NO USE FOR PROFESSIONAL ATHLETES OR MUSICIANS AMONG THEIR OFFSPRING.

Blue Note

"Motherfucker" is an exceedingly common Milesism used primarily to express ardent admiration. For example: *"...the whole band would just like have an orgasm every time Bird or Diz would play.... Sarah Vaughan was there also, and she's a motherfucker too."*

REMEMBER, THIS IS AMERICA IN THE FIRST HALF OF THE CENTURY. A TIME WHEN MILES'S GRAND-FATHER PURCHASED FIVE HUNDRED ACRES OF LAND IN ARKANSAS ONLY TO BE RUN OFF THAT LAND BY THE *VERY SAME* WHITE FOLKS WHOSE FINANCIAL AFFAIRS HE KEPT IN ORDER. A TIME WHEN ST. LOUIS SAW A RIOT ERUPT WHICH LEFT 40 AFRICAN-AMERICANS DEAD WHILE BLACK SOLDIERS WERE DYING IN EUROPE FOR THE SAKE OF SOMEONE ELSE'S DEMOCRACY. A TIME WHEN THE KU KLUX KLAN WAS FOUR MILLION STRONG.

NOW PICTURE THE GREAT DEPRESSION RAGING ALL AROUND WHILE THE DAVISES FLOURISHED — *BLACK AND BUOYANT* — IN A SEA OF SINKING FORTUNES. IT WASN'T SURPRISING THEN THAT MILES II AND CLEOTA SAW A CAREER IN MUSIC TO BE A STEP BACKWARD, A SURE-FIRE WAY FOR YOUNG MILES TO SHUFFLE BACK DOWN INTO THE DARK, *STEPIN FETCHIT* WORLD THEY DESPISED. DOC DAVIS TOLD MARC CRAWFORD, *"MY FATHER, MILES I, WAS BORN SIX YEARS AFTER EMANCIPATION AND FORBADE ME TO PLAY MUSIC BECAUSE THE ONLY PLACE A NEGRO COULD PLAY THEN WAS IN BARRELHOUSES."*

Blue Note

The Encyclopedia of Black America defines a barrelhouse as *"any good time place."* The origin of the term is obscure, though it may have been derived from the barrels found in saloons and clubs.

THE MUSE, HOWEVER, WAS NOT TO BE DENIED. SO, BETWEEN HORSEBACK RIDING ON HIS FATHER'S FARM, PLAYING FOOTBALL WITH FRIENDS, FIGHTING OCCASIONALLY WHEN SOMEONE CALLED HIM "BUCKWHEAT" BECAUSE HE WAS SO DARK AND SKINNY, DODGING THE DISAPPROVING GLANCES OF HIS MOTHER CLEOTA, AND LISTENING TO HIS FATHER'S ORATIONS ON RACE, PRIDE, AND THE HARD LINE OF MARCUS GARVEY, YOUNG MILES WAS SECRETLY SEDUCED BY **"HARLEM RHYTHMS."** LOUIE ARMSTRONG, DUKE ELLINGTON, COUNT BASIE, BESSIE SMITH, JIMMIE LUNCEFORD, HARRY JAMES, AND LIONEL HAMPTON PLAYED ON THE RADIO EVERY MORNING AND MADE MILES LATE FOR SCHOOL ALMOST EVERY DAY.

"...I HAD TO HEAR THAT SHOW, MAN, HAD TO."

BY AGE NINE OR SO, MILES STARTED TAKING MUSIC LESSONS. BY AGE TWELVE THE MUSIC WAS ALL UP IN HIS BONES. FINALLY, BY MILES'S THIRTEENTH BIRTHDAY, MRS. DAVIS BOWED BEFORE THE INEVITABLE AND DECIDED TO BUY HIM A...

...violin!

FORTUNATELY, HIS DAD — THE UNWITTING VOICE OF HIPNESS — INTERVENED AND BOUGHT THE BOY A TRUMPET...

...AND NOW THE BOY COULD *BLOW*.

Blue Note

There is little evidence to suggest that the elder Miles had any idea that he was equipping his son to play in some of the biggest, finest, *motherfuckin'est* barrelhouses in the land, from Huff's Beer Garden to Birdland to Carnegie Hall.

MAKIN' MILES...

WITH THE HORN, THE FUNDAMENTAL ELEMENTS OF THE MILES TO COME WERE ALMOST ALL IN PLACE. HE WAS ALREADY A BOY INHABITED BY HIS FATHER'S TEMPER — AN AMBIENT ANGER AT ONCE TEMPERED AND INFORMED BY SENSITIVITY AND INTELLIGENCE — AN ANGER WHICH WOULD GROW TO BETRAY BOTH. A BOY ENCHANTED BY HIS UNCLE FERD'S BRILLIANCE, PENCHANT FOR FINE CLOTHES AND BEAUTIFUL WOMEN, BY HIS WORLDLINESS AND WORLD TRAVELS. A BOY HAUNTED BY ARKANSAS NIGHTS ON HIS GRANDFATHER'S FARM — OF WALKS DOWN DARK ROADS WITH MUSIC FROM NIGHT SERVICES, THAT KIND OF BLUE, *"CHURCH, BACK-ROAD FUNK KIND OF THING,"* THICKENING THE AIR AND SEEPING INTO HIS SOUL.

BUT ONE CRITICAL ELEMENT WAS STILL MISSING. MR. ELWOOD BUCHANAN — TEACHER.

A HORNMAN IN THE MORE UNDERSTATED, BIX BEIDERBECK TRADITION, BUCHANAN DIDN'T HAVE MUCH USE FOR THE BOLD QUICKSILVER FIREBREATHERS OF THE DAY, SUCH AS LOUIE ARMSTRONG. INSTEAD, HE EMBRACED A LIGHTER, MORE LYRICAL APPROACH TO THE MUSIC. IT IS NOT SURPRISING, THEN, TO DISCOVER THAT ONE DAY BUCHANAN STOPPED THE SCHOOL BAND IN MID-SOUSA TO RIP ALL THAT HARRY JAMES VIBRATO OUT OF YOUNG MILES'S HORN.

"LOOK HERÉ, MILES, STOP SHAKING THOSE NOTES. YOU'RE GOING TO BE SHAKING ENOUGH WHEN YOU GET OLD."

TO BE SINGLED OUT THIS WAY EMBARRASSED MILES BECAUSE HE JUST *KNEW* THAT HE WAS SWINGIN'. YET DROPPING THAT SHAKY HARRY JAMES THANG MARKED THE BIRTH OF, PERHAPS, THE MOST DISTINCTIVE VOICE IN THE HISTORY OF JAZZ. BY THE TIME MILES REACHED HIGH SCHOOL HE WAS PLAYING PRETTY WELL, AND HE JOINED THE HIGH SCHOOL BAND AS ITS YOUNGEST MEMBER. HE STUDIED HARD, DEVOURING THEORY BOOKS, AND LEARNING TO PLAY CHROMATIC SCALES.

ALTHOUGH YOUNG MILES WAS NOT A BRILLIANT TECHNI-
CIAN, EVERYONE ALWAYS SEEMED TO LIKE HIS TONE.
AND HIS COMMITMENT TO HIS MUSIC WAS BEYOND
QUESTION; IT WAS, IN FACT, APPROACHED ONLY BY HIS
GROWING COMMITMENT TO HIS LOOK.

MILES STYLES

THE BOY WAS HIP. BROOKS BROTHERS SUITS. BUTCHER
BOY SHOES. HIGH-DRAPED PANTS. HIGH TAB COLLARS.
CLEAN AS A....

EAST ST. LOUIS WAS AT THE CROSSROADS OF A VERY
HAPPENING MUSIC SCENE. ALONG WITH A BEVY OF
HOME-GROWN JAZZMEN, AND TRUMPETERS IN PARTICU-
LAR, LIKE LEVI MADDISON, HAROLD "SHORTY" BAKER,
DEWEY JACKSON, MOUSE RANDOLPH, SLEEPY TOMLIN,
AND CLARK TERRY, BANDS FROM NEW YORK, NEW
ORLEANS, AND KANSAS CITY REGULARLY WORKED THE
ST. LOUIS CIRCUIT.

THAT WAS THE SCENE FOR MILES.

AT AGE FIFTEEN, MILES MET THE TRUMPETER, CLARK
TERRY, THEN TWENTY-ONE. INTRODUCED TO TERRY AT A
HIGH SCHOOL FUNCTION BY HIS SECOND TEACHER,
GUSTAV, MILES WAS IMMEDIATELY IMPRESSED BY
TERRY'S FAST PLAYING AND HIS PROFOUND HIPNESS.

TERRY "WAS WEARING HIP BUTCHER BOY SHOES AND A BAD HAT COCKED ACE-DEUCE. I TOLD HIM I COULD...TELL HE WAS A TRUMPET PLAYER BY THE HIP SHIT HE WAS WEARING."

AS CLARK TERRY LIKES TO TELL IT, MILES STARTED IN WITH A MILLION QUESTIONS — HOW DO I DO THIS, MR. TERRY? HOW DO I DO THAT, MR. TERRY? MR. TERRY? BUT TERRY'S INTEREST WAS FOCUSED ON SOME PRETTY YOUNG GIRLS BY A MAYPOLE. SO, IN ANSWER TO THE EAGER, FLEDGLING HORNBLOWER'S QUESTIONS, TERRY SAID SIMPLY, "GET LOST, KID."

DISAPPOINTED BUT NOT DISCOURAGED, MILES VOWED IN TIME TO OUTPLAY AND, MOREOVER, TO OUTHIP CLARK TERRY. THE NEXT YEAR WOULD SEE HIM MAKING INROADS INTO THE ST. LOUIS JAZZ SCENE. MILES AND HIS BEST FRIEND, DUKE BROOKS, PUT TOGETHER A LITTLE GROUP AND PLAYED GIGS, FROM HUFF'S BEER GARDEN TO CONSIDERABLY LESS SWINGIN' CHURCH AFFAIRS. MILES EVEN PLAYED IN BROOKLYN (BROOKLYN, ILLINOIS, THAT IS) AND PLEASED THE CROWDS OF COLOR WHO LIKED THEIR MUSIC STRAIGHT UP, ON TIME, AND HAD NO TIME FOR MR. JIVEASS NON-PLAYIN' WANNABEE UP'NSTAGE TRYIN' TO GET OVER'N WASTIN' MY TIME. AND SLOWLY, MILES BEGAN TO MAKE SOME- THING OF A NAME FOR HIMSELF.

"We shall soon have our Storm Troopers in America!"
— HITLER

What do YOU say, AMERICA?

THE EUROPEAN WAR HOVERED OVER THE AMERICAN
CONSCIOUSNESS, AND ON DECEMBER 6, 1941, IT
ERUPTED WITH SUDDEN VIOLENCE INTO THE SECOND
WORLD WAR. AS MANY TALENTED PLAYERS WERE
DRAWN INTO THE ARMED FORCES, THOSE WHO WERE
LEFT BEHIND FOUND ENHANCED OPPORTUNITIES TO
MOVE ONTO THE BANDSTANDS. THIS FACT DID NOT
MAKE MILES'S EARLY CAREER, BUT IT DIDN'T HURT IT
EITHER. AND IT WAS IN 1941 THAT MILES LANDED HIS
FIRST REGULAR JOB AS A TRUMPET PLAYER.

THE GROUP WAS CALLED EDDIE RANDLE'S BLUE
DEVILS, "THE ONLY BAND IN TOWN" ACCORDING TO
MILES.

BLUE NOTE

Miles was never reluctant to state his musical tastes. At the age of
fifteen he and his boy Bobby Danzig, also a trumpet player, would
run from club to club — gig-hopping — and he or Bobby might say,
*Let's get out of here, man. Look how the trumpet player's stand-
ing. You know that motherfucker can't play!* Later in life, his *Down
Beat Magazine* Blindfold Tests, in which he would critique the
music of his contemporaries, would become legendary. On one
occasion his views were so harsh that Leonard Feather felt compelled to preface the column by stating that Miles *"...is unusually
selective in his listening habits. This attitude should not be inter-
preted as reflecting any general misanthropy."*

ONE DAY WHILE HE WAS RAVING OVER THE BLUE
DEVILS, MILES'S FIRST GIRLFRIEND, IRENE, DARED HIM
TO AUDITION FOR THE BAND. MILES TOOK TO DARES
LIKE A FISH TO WATER, SO HE AUDITIONED. AND HE
WAS HIRED.

MILES, NOW A BLUE DEVIL, BEGAN TO PLAY LIKE HELL. SO WHEN CLARK TERRY HEARD THIS BAD-ASSED NEW TRUMPET PLAYER FLYING ALL OVER EDDIE RANDLE'S BLUE DEVILS RHUMBOOGIE ORCHESTRA LESS THAN A YEAR LATER, HE SAID, "AREN'T YOU-?", MILES REPLIED, "YEAH,... YOU WOULDN'T EVEN TALK TO ME WHEN I FIRST MET YOU OVER IN CARBONDALE; I'M THE LITTLE DUDE YOU SHINED ON OVER THERE."

THEREAFTER, MILES AND TERRY BECAME CLOSE FRIENDS. IT LIFTED HIS CONFIDENCE TO BE HELD IN SUCH HIGH REGARD BY ONE OF HIS !DOLS. IT ALSO ALLOWED HIM MUCH GREATER ACCESS TO THE ST. LOUIS JAZZ SCENE, FROM SMOKY CLUBS TO SHOW-BOATS BALLASTED BY WOMEN AND WHISKEY.

UPON GRADUATING FROM HIGH SCHOOL IN JUNE 1944
MILES JOINED UP WITH **ADAM LAMBERT'S SIX BROWN
CATS**. WITH THEM HE TOURED OUTSIDE ST. LOUIS FOR
THE FIRST TIME. HE DID NOT, HOWEVER, LIKE THE
MUSIC THEY WERE PLAYING, SO WHEN THE BAND WENT
ON TO CHICAGO, MILES WENT BACK HOME.

THIS TURNED OUT TO BE ONE OF THE BEST MOVES
THAT MILES EVER MADE, FOR HE RETURNED TO FIND
THAT **BILLY ECKSTINE,** KNOWN IN HIPPER CIRCLES AS
"MR. B" OR "B", WOULD BE IN TOWN. AND B'S BAND
FEATURED SOME OF THE *HOTTEST* YOUNG
MUSICIANS IN JAZZ.

CLARK
TERRY

AS
MILES TELLS IT, ONE
EVENING, TRUMPET IN HAND, HE
BOPPED DOWN TO JORDAN
CHAMBER'S RIVIERA CLUB TO
CHECK OUT B'S BAND. AS SOON
AS HE ENTERED THE CLUB HE
WAS ACCOSTED BY A HEP CAT IN
A FRENZY ASKING HIM IF HE HAD A UNION
CARD. UPON SAYING YES HE WAS
WHISKED ONTO THE STAGE, AND FOUND HIMSELF PLAY-
ING WITH NONE OTHER CHARLIE PARKER AND DIZZY
GILLESPIE — *FIERCE, TERRIBLE, PEERLESS* NEW CATS
BASED IN NEW YORK CITY. (THAT HEP CAT, AS IT TURNED
OUT, WAS DIZZY HIMSELF.)

Blue Note

Billy Eckstine recalls Miles's two week gig with the band a little differently. *"Miles used to follow us around in St. Louis. He used to ask to sit in with the band. I used to let him so as not to hurt his feelings, because then Miles was awful."*

AFTER PLAYING WITH MR. B'S BAND,
THE ATTRACTION OF ANY PLACE ON EARTH OTHER THAN
NEW YORK WAS SUDDENLY AND IRRETRIEVABLY LOST. SO
WHEN MRS. DAVIS INSISTED THAT HER SON GO TO FISK
UNIVERSITY, AND HELD OUT THE FISK JUBILEE SINGERS
AS A CARROT-ON-A-STICK, MILES ALMOST CERTAINLY
BROKE INTO A CHORUS OF EXPLETIVES MEANT TO CONVEY
HIS PROFOUND LACK OF INTEREST.

Blue Note

In fairness to Mama Davis, who at this point seems hopelessly
square, we must point out that she was hip enough to have bought
Miles his very first Duke Ellington and Art Tatum albums. And
unbeknown to Miles until later in life, she would also, from time to
time, feel the spirit and lay down some pretty kickin' blues riffs on
the piano.

e quel. Dal vivo fonte de la tua bontate, ch'ogni gente arrichisce in ogni etat

& ogni mente paſ— ce, quanto in terra tra noi more e rinaſ—

Anto e quel. Dal vivo fonte de la tua bontate, ch'ogni gente arrichisce in ogni

corpo & ogni mente paſ— ce, quanto in terra tra noi more e rinaſ—

orna et ac- cende d'alta caritate, co- ſa non è ch'ign

FORTUNE WAS KIND, HOWEVER, FOR THE JULLIARD SCHOOL OF MUSIC WAS IN NEW YORK. BY ATTENDING *IT*, MILES COULD PLACATE HIS PARENTS *AND* BE AMIDST THOSE IN THE VANGUARD OF MODERN JAZZ. SO IN 1944 MILES ARRIVED IN NEW YORK, PASSED HIS AUDITIONS WITH A RENDITION OF *YOUTH DAUNTLESS* (INDEED), AND SPENT HIS DAYS STUDYING MUSIC THEORY AND CLASSICAL MUSIC. BUT BY NIGHT, YOUNG MILES WAS...

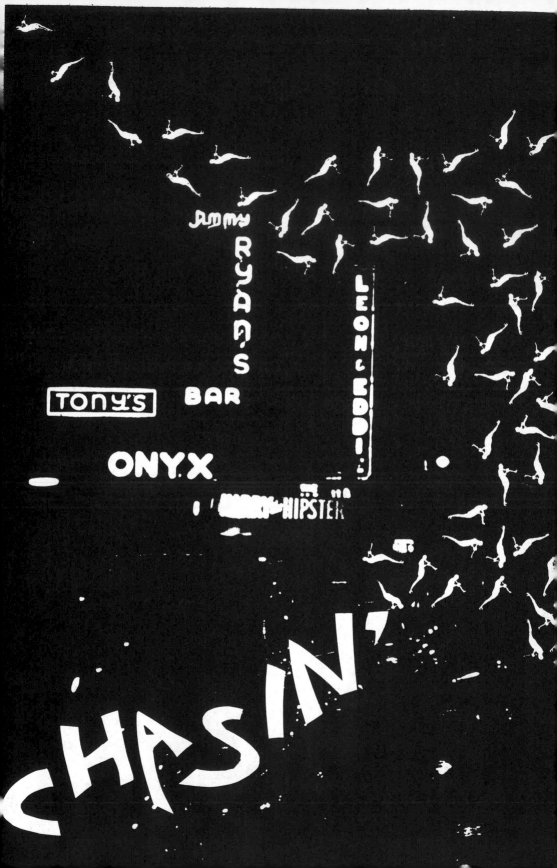

MILES ARRIVED IN NEW YORK CITY
AND STARTED COMB-
ING THE CLUBS EVERY
NIGHT IN SEARCH OF
THE ELUSIVE BIRD.
EVERY NIGHT HE TOOK IN
FANTASTIC
MUSIC AS HIS
SEARCH
TOOK HIM
TO PLACES
LIKE MINTON'S,
OR CLARK
MONROE'S

UPTOWN
HOUSE IN
HARLEM;
THE THREE
DEUCES, THE
ONYX, OR
KELLY'S STABLE
ON THE STREET,
(52ND STREET).
BUT EVEN THOUGH
BIRD AND DIZZY
WERE FAST BE-
COMING LEGENDS,
THEY WERE STILL
RELATIVELY DIFFICULT
TO FIND.

FINALLY, AFTER A COUPLE OF
WEEKS, MILES TRACKED DOWN
DIZZY GILLESPIE. HE WAS
DELIGHTED TO FIND THAT DIZ
REMEMBERED HIM. BUT
TO HIS DISMAY DIZ
HADN'T SEEN BIRD
EITHER.

ONE NIGHT
MILES RAN
INTO

COLEMAN
"BEAN"
HAWKINS,
ONE OF HIS
JAZZ HEROES.
MILES TOLD
BEAN OF HIS
QUEST.
BEAN
LAUGHED
PERHAPS
A BIT
TOO

KNOWINGLY
FOR MILES'S
TASTE, AND TOLD
THE YOUNG-
STER TO STAY
IN JULLIARD
AND NOT TO
GET MIXED UP
WITH THE LIKES
OF CHARLIE PARKER.

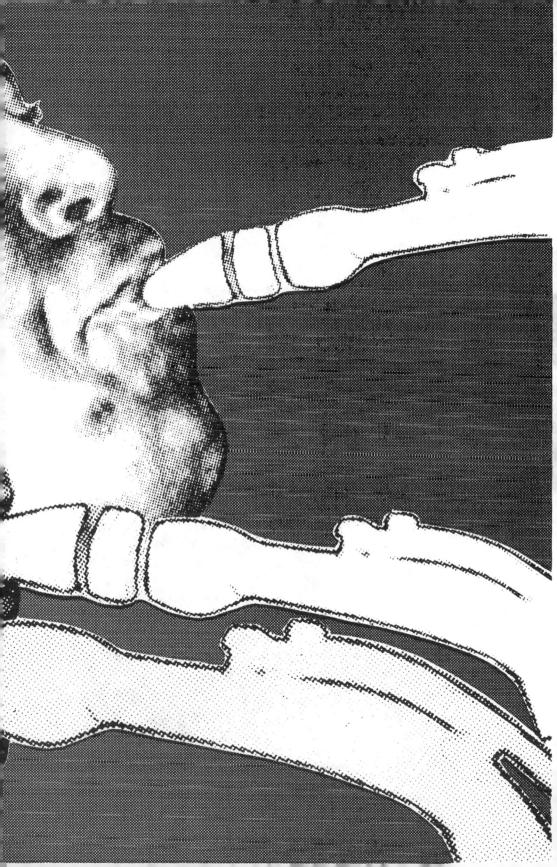

Blue Note

Charlie *"Yardbird"* Parker was at the head of the bebop revolution. Recognized as one of the greatest, if not the greatest improviser in the history of jazz, Bird was one of the true musical geniuses of the twentieth century. But, he was also a man of alarming appetites, a man capable of tremendous greed and egoism. A heroin addict since the age of fifteen, he was a master hustler. And although he used those around him without apology, he got away with it because he was the *greatest player alive.* Down the road Miles would go on to say, *"...Bird was a greedy mother-fucker, like most geniuses are. He wanted everything. And when he was desperate for a fix of heroin, man, Bird would do any-thing to get it."*

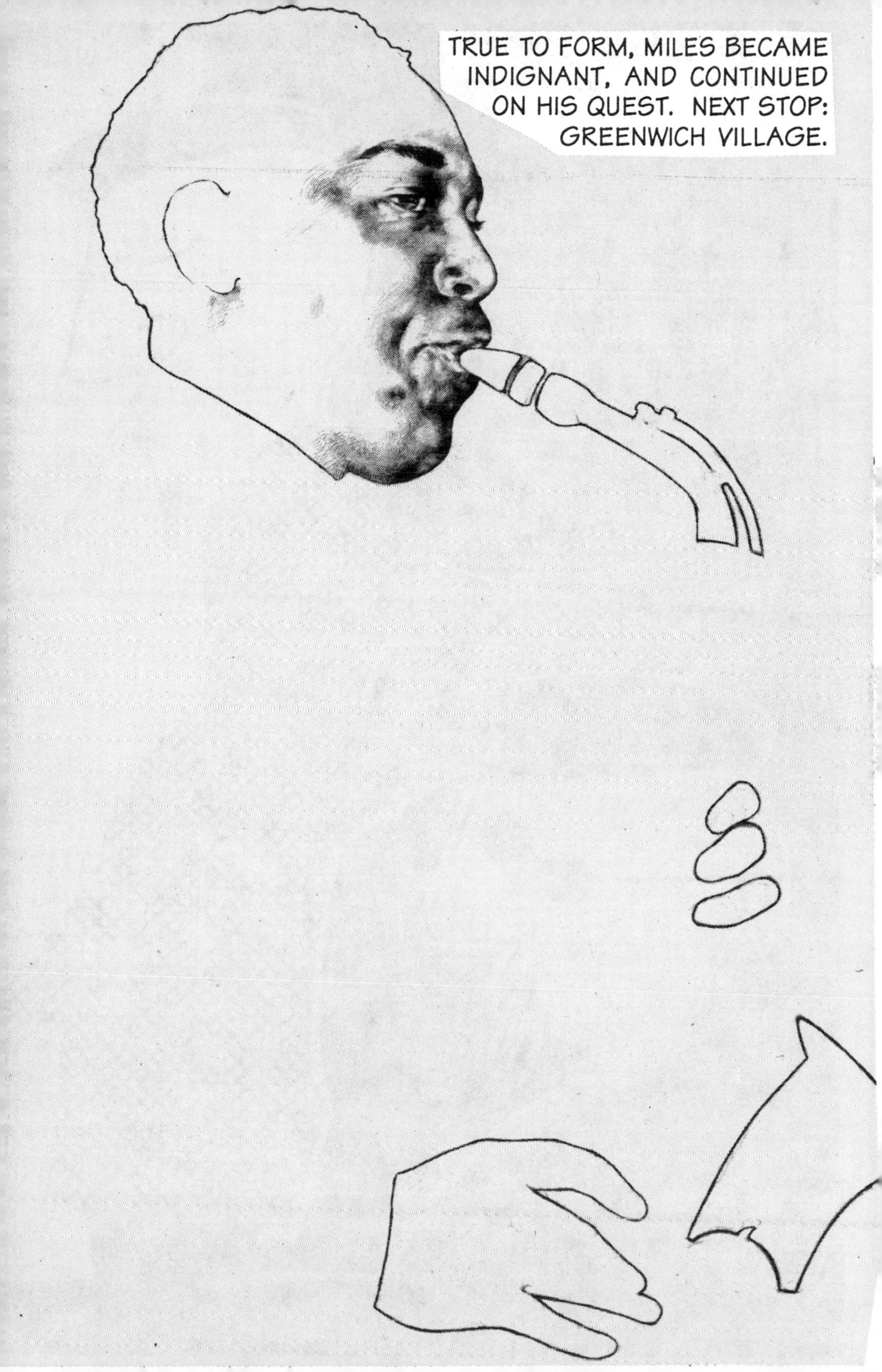
TRUE TO FORM, MILES BECAME INDIGNANT, AND CONTINUED ON HIS QUEST. NEXT STOP: GREENWICH VILLAGE.

ARTISTS.
WRITERS.
LONG-HAIRED, BEARDED,
BEATNIK POETS, ALL-DAY-
KEROUAC-ING,
ENSCONCED IN VILLAGE
CAFES, SMOKING CIGARETTES,
PONDERING THE
UNANSWERABLE,
AND LISTENING
TO JAZZ.
TOO COOL.

BUT NO BIRD.

FINALLY MILES FOUND HIS WAY TO A GIG AT THE
HEATWAVE ON 145TH STREET IN HARLEM.

"HEY MILES, I HEARD YOU BEEN LOOKIN' FOR ME." IT
WAS BIRD. IT WAS *REALLY* BIRD, GREETING MILES
WARMLY, INVITING HIM TO STAY FOR THE SHOW, GOING
BACK TO MILES'S BOARDING HOUSE WITH HIM, SPENDING
THE NIGHT TALKING ABOUT EVERYTHING AND NOTHING,
MOVING IN THE NEXT DAY, ROOMING WITH HIM FOR A
COUPLE OF MONTHS, AND STAYING ON UNTIL
MILES GREW TIRED OF HIS APPETITES, TIRED
OF BEING HUSTLED IN HIS OWN HOME.

THINGS WERE MUCH BETTER ON THE BAND-
STAND, AND MILES SOON BEGAN PLAYING DATES
WITH BIRD AND DIZ. HE WAS ENCOURAGED, INSPIRED BY
BIRD. BUT, MOREOVER, HE WAS AWESTRUCK,
AND HE USED TO QUIT EVERY NIGHT.

MILES WOULD ASK, *"WHAT DO YOU NEED ME FOR?"*
BIRD'S RESPONSE WAS SIMPLE: *"DON'T BE AFRAID. JUST
GO AHEAD AND PLAY."*

BUT WHILE BIRD WAS HIS INSPIRATION,
DIZZY WAS HIS TEACHER. DIZZY TAUGHT MILES HOW
TO PLAY THE PIANO, AND HOW TO USE IT TO FIND
THE PRETTY NOTES THAT ELUDE THOSE WHO NEVER
STRAY FROM THEIR OWN INSTRUMENT. BUT
MILES WAS NOT A CLONE OF DR. DIZ.

ONE DAY MILES ASKED DIZZY, "WHY CAN'T I PLAY
HIGH LIKE YOU?"

"BECAUSE YOU DON'T HEAR UP THERE," WAS DIZZY'S
RESPONSE.

SO, WHILE MOST JAZZ AFICIONADOS AGREE THAT
WITHOUT DIZZY THERE WOULD HAVE BEEN
NO MILES, IT WAS CLEAR FROM
THE OUTSET THAT MILES'S
VOICE WOULD BE
HIS OWN.

1945 - 1947 WOULD PROVE TO BE PIVOTAL YEARS IN MILES'S MUSICAL DEVELOPMENT. NOW A PART OF THE JAZZ SCENE'S INNER CIRCLE BY VIRTUE OF HIS ASSOCIATION WITH THE GURUS OF BEBOP, HE WAS FOREVER IN THE PRESENCE OF EAGER-TO-JAM YOUNG CATS LIKE...

max roach
bud powell
fats *fat girl* navarro
thelonious monk
charles mingus

...AS WELL AS, OLDER, ESTABLISHED CATS LIKE COLEMAN HAWKINS, BILLY ECKSTINE, EDDIE "LOCKJAW" DAVIS, AND ILLINOIS JACQUET. (MILES WAS A SIDEMAN ON A NUMBER OF RECORDING DATES WITH MANY OF THOSE LISTED ABOVE.)

Blue Note

Miles was ultimately to leave Julliard in the fall of 1945 to pursue a Ph.D. from the *"University of Bebop under the tutelage of Professors Bird and Diz."* Aside from the prospect of enduring the racism of the symphonic establishment, playing two notes every ninety bars in an orchestra just wasn't Miles's style. And those *clothes*...

THESE YEARS
WOULD ALSO SEE THE
GREAT BOP ALLIANCE OF
CHARLIE PARKER AND DIZZY GILLESPIE
COME TO AN END — BIRD'S EXCESSES AND
IRRESPONSIBILITY DROVE DIZZY TO QUIT THE BAND.
BIRD DECIDED TO REPLACE DIZZY'S HYPER-KINETIC
BOP SOUND WITH A *DIFFERENT* SOUND, AND MILES
DAVIS WAS CALLED ON TO STEP INTO DIZZY
GILLESPIE'S BOP-BAD SHOES. IN APRIL OF 1947 THE
FIRST, AND PERHAPS BEST, OF THE CHARLIE PARKER
QUINTETS CAME TOGETHER FEATURING CHARLIE
PARKER ON ALTO SAXOPHONE, MILES DAVIS ON
TRUMPET, AND MAX ROACH ON DRUMS.

MILES HAD ARRIVED. HE WAS PLAYING WITH THE
PREMIER QUINTET IN THE LAND AND WAS THE ENVY
OF ORNITHOLOGISTS EVERYWHERE.

Blue Note

or•ni•thol•o•gy \ n \ a branch of zoology dealing with the study of birds.

MANY CRITICS AND MUSICIANS, HOWEVER, WERE HOSTILE TO BIRD'S REPLACEMENT OF DIZZY'S BRASS PYROMANIA WITH MILES' MORE SUBDUED SOUND. BUT, WHILE BIRD AND DIZ PLAYED BRILLIANTLY TOGETHER, THEY ALSO CIRCLED EACH OTHER PERHAPS A BIT TOO TIGHTLY, TOO QUICKLY, LIKE TWO SPEEDING JAZZATOMIC PARTICLES CONSTRAINED BY EACH OTHER'S GRAVITY.

BUT, OFFSET BY MILES'S VOICE, BIRD WAS ABLE TO
STRETCH OUT AND TO EXPLORE MUSICAL PLACES HE
COULD NOT EXPLORE BEFORE. AND YOUNG MILES SAW
THE BEAUTY OF FIRE AND ICE — A FEATURE WHICH WOULD
BECOME THE HALLMARK OF HIS GREAT COMBOS TO COME.

MILESTONES 1947
**• IN AUGUST MILES LEADS HIS FIRST SESSION
ON THE SAVOY LABEL — THE *MILES DAVIS ALL-
STARS*, FEATURING FOUR ORIGINAL COMPOSI-
TIONS, AND CHARLIE PARKER AS THE SECOND
HORN. • 1947 ALSO SEES MILES WIN THE
ESQUIRE NEW STAR AWARD FOR TRUMPET, AND
TIE DIZZY GILLESPIE FOR THE *DOWN BEAT*
KUDOS. • MILES MEETS THE COMPOSER/AR-
RANGER GIL EVANS AND PLANTS THE SEED
FOR MANY COLLABORATIONS TO COME.**

MILES'S MUSICAL WORLD, HOWEVER, WAS NOT ALWAYS
IN TUNE. PLAYING WITH BIRD WAS, WELL, *PLAYING
WITH THE BIRD.*

*"...ANYTHING MIGHT HAPPEN
MUSICALLY WHEN YOU WERE
PLAYING WITH BIRD...."*

BUT *THE GREAT BIRD WAS AN ERRATIC FLYER.* WHEN A LEADER FAILS TO PAY HIS SIDEMEN ON TIME, IF AT ALL, FAILS TO SHOW UP AT GIGS, OR SHOWS UP IMPAIRED BY BOOZE AND HEROIN, THEN HE WILL LOSE THOSE SIDEMEN. EVEN IF THAT LEADER IS THE GREAT CHARLIE PARKER.

Blue Note

Miles was a proud little mother and he refused to be dissed by Bird or anyone else. But Miles was also a reluctant little *father*. And he needed his money to feed his high school sweetheart, Irene Birth, and his two children, Cheryl and Gregory, who were living with Miles in New York.

1948 CAUGHT GIL EVANS LEAVING CLAUDE THORNHILL'S BIG BAND TO EXPLORE HIS TALENTS WITH NEW MUSICIANS, AND MILES DAVIS ON THE BRINK OF THE SAME. THAT SUMMER THE TWO CAME TOGETHER IN A UNION WHICH BEGAT MILES'S NONET, A NINE-PIECE BAND WHICH AUGMENTED THE STANDARD BOP QUINTET WITH A REED AND THREE BRASS INSTRUMENTS. AND FROM THE UNION OF THE NONET CAME MILES'S FIRST MAJOR CONTRIBUTION TO THE MUSIC:

THE BIRTH OF THE COOL

Blue Note

Bebop was firemusic. Too-hot-for-rcd *blue-hot* firemusic. Bebop was polyrhythmic jet fuel flights of concentrated soulbursts. Bebop was a dizbird skydancing toward critical. But The Birth draped the music in The Cool, gently arced her away from the chaos and closer to the Mystery, closer to a different kind of blue.

FOR TWO WEEKS IN SEPTEMBER 1948 THE MILES DAVIS NONET PLAYED THE *ROYAL ROOST*, KNOWN BY HEP CATS AS THE *METROPOLITAN BOPERA HOUSE*. THE NONET WAS THEN INACTIVE UNTIL JANUARY 1949.

IN THE MEANTIME, BIRD AND COMPANY WERE PLAYING THE ROOST AS WELL. AND BECAUSE THE GIGS WERE BEING BROADCAST (UNDER THE AUSPICES OF SYMPHONY SID TORIN, THE *ALL-NIGHT, ALL FRANTIC ONE*) —

"I NEVER DID LIKE THAT MOTHERFUCKER."

— MILES DAVIS WAS NOW TURNING INTO A HOUSEHOLD NAME.

ONE EVENING, **DUKE ELLINGTON** —

"...THE MASTER HIMSELF"

— PERSONALLY INVITED MILES TO JOIN HIS FAMOUS ORCHESTRA. MILES, HOWEVER, WAS JUST BEGINNING TO FIND HIS VOICE, AND HE HAD NO DESIRE TO LOSE IT IN THE SWING-SWIRL OF A BIG BAND. BUT TALK ABOUT *GROOVIN' HIGH* — AFTER ELLINGTON'S INVITATION YOU COULDN'T TELL MILES THAT HE WASN'T A *TERRIBLE MOTHERFUCKER!* AND WHEN MILES FINALLY LEFT BIRD IN DECEMBER 1948, HIS CONFIDENCE WAS AT AN ALL-TIME HIGH.

MILESTONES 1949

• IN JANUARY MILES TAKES THE NONET INTO THE STUDIO TO RECORD THE FIRST OF THE *BIRTH OF THE COOL* SESSIONS. • HE IS NAMED TO THE *METRONOME ALL STARS* AND RECORDS A SESSION WITH DIZZY GILLESPIE THEN FLIES LICK-FOR-LICK WITH THE PROFESSOR AND WINS THE RESPECT OF THE DIZZY DIE-HARDS. • AND FOR THE FIRST TIME IN HIS LIFE MILES PACKS UP AND TAKES HIS HORN TO PARIS...IN *APRIL*.

EN PARIS...

...MILES QUIETLY PROFILED WHILE SIPPING CAFE AU LAIT AVEC LES AVANT-GARDES.

—JEAN-PAUL SARTRE AND PABLO PICASSO...

EN PARIS...

...MILES WAS THE HIT OF THE PARIS JAZZ FESTIVAL.

"EVEN THE BAND AND THE MUSIC WE PLAYED SOUNDED BETTER OVER THERE."

EN PARIS...

...MILES WAS KING OF THE WORLD.

"THE ONLY OTHER TIME I FELT THAT GOOD WAS WHEN I FIRST HEARD BIRD AND DIZ...."

EN PARIS...

...MILES MET A MADEMOISELLE.

"WHO IS SHE?"

"WELL YOU KNOW [JULIETTE GRECO'S] ONE OF THOSE EXISTENTIALISTS."

"MAN, FUCK ALL THAT KIND OF SHIT. I DON'T CARE WHAT SHE IS. THAT GIRL IS BEAUTIFUL AND I WANT TO MEET HER."

ET EN PARIS...

...MILES FELL IN LOVE.

"JULIETTE AND I USED TO WALK DOWN BY THE SEINE TOGETHER, HOLDING HANDS AND KISSING, LOOKING INTO EACH OTHER'S EYES, AND KISSING SOME MORE, AND SQUEEZING EACH OTHER'S HANDS. IT WAS LIKE MAGIC."

AH, PARIS, VILLE D'AMOUR...

WHEN MILES FINALLY FLEW HOME, HE STEPPED OFF THE PLANE, AND QUIETLY SLIPPED INTO A DEEP BLUE FUNK. NEW YORK'S STYLE OF AMBIENT RACISM DIDN'T *SEEM* TO EXIST IN PARIS, AND SUDDENLY IT WAS FAR MORE DIFFICULT TO ENDURE. WHITE MUSICIANS WERE COPYING HIS *BIRTH OF THE COOL* SOUND, AND WERE GETTING MOST OF THE CLUB DATES AND RECOGNITION. AND TO TOP IT OFF, MILES MISSED JULIETTE GRECO MORE THAN WAS HIP TO REVEAL. PERHAPS HE SHOULD HAVE LISTENED TO SARTRE AND MARRIED HER. PERHAPS IT WOULD HAVE STAVED OFF THE RELENTLESS NAUSEA...

PARKER'S MOOD

IN CERTAIN JAZZ CIRCLES, A SECRET CODE WAS USED TO
IDENTIFY MEMBERS OF A SELECT SOCIETY. THE CODE
WAS THE FIRST THREE NOTES OF CHARLIE PARKER'S
PARKER'S MOOD. THE SOCIETY WAS MADE UP OF HEROIN
ADDICTS.

HEROIN USE WAS COMMON IN THE JAZZ WORLD,
PARTICULARLY IN THE LAND OF BOP, AND THOSE WHO
USED IT RAN LIKE A WHO'S WHO OF JAZZ:

CHARLIE PARKER	BILLY HOLIDAY
ART BLAKEY	CHET BAKER
SONNY ROLLINS	FATS NAVARRO
DEXTER GORDON	BUD POWELL
STAN GETZ	TADD DAMERON
GERRY MULLIGAN	SONNY STITT
RED RODNEY	FREDDIE WEBSTER

MILES, NOW TWENTY-THREE, HAD SPENT FOUR HEROIN-
FREE YEARS WITH BIRD. BUT AFTER HE RETURNED FROM
PARIS, MILES, LIKE THE OTHERS, WAS STEADY WHISTLING
PARKER'S MOOD.

MEANWHILE, THE JAZZ SCENE IN NEW YORK WAS DRYING
UP, AND THE STREET WAS CLOSING DOWN. IN 1950
DIZZY'S ORCHESTRA DISBANDED, AS DID COUNTLESS
OTHERS.

AND IN 1950 MILES LED THE LAST BOP BAND ON 52ND
STREET AS THE CLUBS GAVE WAY TO OFFICE BUILDINGS
AND BECAME A PART OF LOST NEW YORK.

BEFORE TAKING TO THE NEEDLE, MILES WAS FAST
BECOMING *THE* YOUNG FORCE ON THE SCENE. HE HAD
STARTED TO REDEFINE THE STANDARD FOR EXCELLENCE
ON THE HORN. BEBOP BAD WAS HIGH AND FAST, AND THE
HIGHER AND FASTER YOU WENT THE BADDER YOU WERE.
NOW *IDEAS* AND *TONE* WERE COOLER THAN THE SPEED OF
LIGHT. AND WHILE MILES WAS STILL IN A CREATIVE
GROOVE, HE WAS SINKING FAST, PLAYING ERRATICALLY,
MISSING GIGS, DISAPPEARING FOR WEEKS AT A TIME,
AND, WHILE OUT IN CALIFORNIA WITH B'S BAND, HE WAS
BUSTED FOR HEROIN POSSESSION.

THE BAD PRESS SURROUNDING THE ARREST CAME HARD
AND FAST AND IN 1951 MILES PLAYED CLUB DATES ONLY
SIX OR SEVEN WEEKS OUT OF THE ENTIRE YEAR. (HE WAS
ULTIMATELY ACQUITTED OF ALL DRUG CHARGES BUT THE
DAMAGE HAD BEEN DONE.)

IN SPITE OF ALL THIS, MILES HAD SIGNED A RECORD DEAL
WITH PRESTIGE, AND RECORDED FREQUENTLY.

BUT MILES WAS A JUNKIE — A WEAK, RUNNY NOSED, QUIVERING, CHILL-RACKED, STONE-COLD JUNKIE. AND HIS HABIT WAS COSTING HIM FAR MORE MONEY THAN HE WAS EARNING, SO MILES TOOK TO AN EVEN DARKER TRADITION — PIMPING.

AND SO IT WENT.

THEN, LATE ONE NIGHT IN THE SPRING OF 1953, MILES WAS STANDING OUTSIDE BIRDLAND LOOKING EVERY BIT THE JUNKIE WHEN HE WAS APPROACHED BY **MAX ROACH.** MAX TOOK A GOOD LOOK AT MILES AND SLAPPED TWO CRISP $100 BILLS IN HIS HAND AND TOLD HIM THAT HE WAS *"LOOKING GOOD."*

MAX, WHO HAD BEEN LIKE A BROTHER TO MILES SINCE THE EARLY BIRD DAYS, WAS CLEAN AND TAKING CARE OF HIMSELF, AND HIS GESTURE SO HUMILIATED MILES THAT MILES CALLED HIS FATHER AND RETURNED TO ST. LOUIS TO GET CLEAN. THIS FIRST ATTEMPT WASN'T SUCCESSFUL.

SINCE CHILDHOOD MILES HAD BEEN AVID BOXING FAN, AND IT WAS AFTER MEETING BOXING LEGEND **SUGAR RAY ROBINSON** AND BEING MOVED BY HIS TREMENDOUS DRIVE AND SELF-DISCIPLINE THAT MILES RETURNED TO ST. LOUIS, LOCKED HIMSELF INTO THE GUEST HOUSE ON HIS FATHER'S FARM IN MILLSTADT, AND WENT COLD-TURKEY. AFTER THE CHILLS AND CONVULSIONS, AFTER THE PRE-DEATH RIGOR MORTIS STIFFNESS, AFTER THE PLEASE-LET-ME-DIE PLEAS TO AN INDIFFERENT GOD, MILES KICKED HIS HABIT. AND MILES, ALWAYS THE DEFIANT LONER, KICKED IT *ON HIS OWN.*

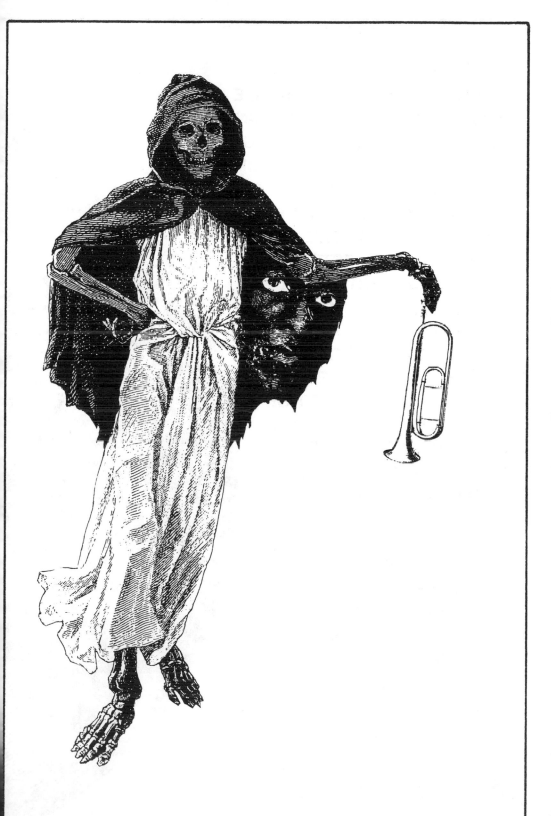

MILESTONES 1955
• THE INCOMPARABLE CHARLIE
"YARDBIRD" PARKER DIES ON
MARCH 12. • MILES HEARS JULIAN
"CANNONBALL" ADDERLY FOR THE
FIRST TIME, AND IS BLOWN AWAY
BY HIS SAXOPHONE BLUES.
• MILES TEARS UP THE
NEWPORT JAZZ FESTIVAL BY
PLAYING, AMONG OTHER
THINGS, MONK'S *ROUND
MIDNIGHT* WITH A MUTE. •
MILES TIES DIZZY GILLESPIE
FOR THE DOWN BEAT
KUDOS. • BOTH PRESTIGE
AND COLUMBIA RECORDS
ARE BIG-TIME COURTIN'
MILES, AND TALKIN' CRAZY
MONEY. • AND IN 1955 MILES
PUTS TOGETHER THE NEW
BOSS COMBO
ON THE SCENE,
THE COMBO THAT
WOULD MAKE HIM
A LEGEND,
FEATURING...

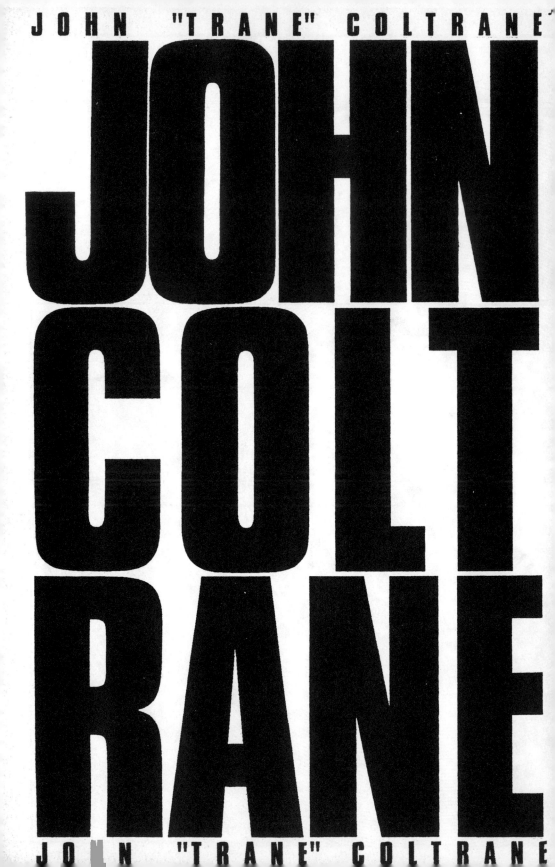

Blue Note

When John Coltrane (Trane) first came onto the scene his sound was considered to be *"strident"* and *"unpleasant"* *"musical non-sense."* Joining Miles gave Trane legitimacy, and within the Davis milieu, Trane was soon to convert the infidels by changing jazz in as basic a way as Charlie Parker and Louie Armstrong had before him. In time he would be deemed The Prophet. Of Coltrane's music Nat Hentoff writes: *"Time. Vast, fierce stretches of time. The music sometimes sounding like the exorcism of a multitude of demons, each one of whom was mightily resisting his expulsion. Yet at other times Coltrane could sound his probes with such gentle luminescence as to fool the voracious spirits, but soon the shaking, smashing, endless battle would begin again."*

SIMPLY PUT, THIS MILES
DAVIS QUINTET WAS THE
HOTTEST COMBO SINCE LOUIE
ARMSTRONG'S HOT FIVE. THE
MUSIC THEY MADE MARKED MILES'S
SECOND LANDMARK ADDITION TO JAZZ,
AND STOOD AS A HIGH WATER MARK IN
THE HISTORY OF THE MUSIC.

THE SOUNDS WERE REVOLU-
TIONARY. MILES'S HORN
HAD

REACHED LYRIC MATURITY,
AND HIS UNIQUE VOICINGS
WERE FULL OF SUBTLETY
AND CONFIDENCE, AND
HIS USE OF SPACE
MORE THAN MADE UP
FOR HIS TECHNICAL
SHORTCOMINGS. SET
AGAINST TRANE'S
SEARCHING, CRAZY-
LAYERED "SHEETS OF
SOUND", AND PUNCTU
ATED BY JOE JONES
"PHILLY LICK" ON THE
DRUMS, THE COMBO
WON INSTANT ACCLAIM.
THEY PACKED CLUBS
WHEREVER THEY
PLAYED.

"THE MUSIC THAT WE WERE PLAYING... WAS SO BAD THAT IT USED TO SEND CHILLS THROUGH ME AT NIGHT...."

TO TOP IT OFF, MILES SIGNED A CONTRACT WITH COLUMBIA RECORDS TO THE TUNE OF $300,000 A YEAR — AN UNHEARD OF SUM FOR A JAZZMAN OF COLOR.

BUT 1955 WAS A YEAR OF GIANT STEPS IN THE AFRICAN-AMERICAN COMMUNITY. IN THE ARTS, MARIAN ANDERSON BECAME THE FIRST AFRICAN-AMERICAN TO APPEAR AT THE METROPOLITAN OPERA AS ULRICA IN VERDI'S UN BALLO IN MASCHERA. ARTHUR MITCHELL BECAME THE FIRST AFRICAN-AMERICAN TO DANCE WITH THE NEW YORK CITY BALLET IN A PRODUCTION OF GEORGE BALANCHINE'S WESTERN SYMPHONY. ON A LARGER SCALE, ROSA PARKS REFUSED TO RELINQUISH HER SEAT TO A WHITE MAN ON A BUS IN MONTGOMERY, ALABAMA UNLEASHING A STORM OF PROTEST THAT WOULD CHANGE THE NATION.

BACK IN NEW YORK THE BOSS COMBO CONTINUED ITS ASCENT.
THAT ASCENT, HOWEVER, WAS FAR FROM SMOOTH. ALTHOUGH THE
GROUP IMMEDIATELY HIT IT OFF — ALL WERE USHERS AT TRANE'S
WEDDING — THEY WOULD BREAK UP AT LEAST FOUR TIMES OVER
THE NEXT TWO YEARS.

THE CENTRAL PROBLEM WAS HEROIN. MILES WAS CLEAN. IT WAS
NOW COLTRANE WHISTLING *PARKER'S MOOD*, SHOWING UP AT GIGS
STRUNG OUT, AND NODDING ON STAGE. AFTER REPEATED *I-BEEN-
THERE-I-KNOW* ATTEMPTS TO URGE TRANE TO STRAIGHTEN UP AND
FLY RIGHT, MILES DID WHAT SEEM INCONCEIVABLE TO FANS OF
THE MUSIC TODAY — HE FIRED JOHN COLTRANE TWICE IN 1956,
AND ONCE AGAIN IN 1957. MILES LOVED TRANE, CALLING HIM A
BEAUTIFUL, REALLY SWEET, SPIRITUAL KIND OF GUY WHO LIVED TO
MAKE MUSIC. BUT, AT THE TIME, TRANE WAS A PATHETIC JUNKY IN
DIRTY CLOTHES SABOTAGING BOTH HIMSELF AND HIS MUSIC.

FINALLY, IN 1957, TRANE WENT COLD TURKEY. LIKE MILES, HE DID IT
ALONE. IN A DOWNBEAT HE WAS CAUSING A SENSATION AT THE
FIVE SPOT WITH THELONIOUS MONK, AND MILES WAS IN THE
AUDIENCE EVERY CHANCE HE GOT.

MEANWHILE, MILES WAS RECORDING GREAT MUSIC WITH GIL
EVANS, PLAYING AND JET SETTING, LIVING LARGE AND CRUISING
IN HIS WHITE MERCEDES. HE EVEN RECORDED A
SOUNDTRACK IN PARIS FOR LOUIS MALLE'S FILM *ASCENSEUR POUR
L'ECHAFAUD*. ALL THE WHILE HE WAS CULTIVATING A DREAM. IN
DECEMBER OF 1957 THAT DREAM CAME TRUE. TRANE WAS BACK,
AND CANNONBALL ADDERLY HAD SIGNED ON.

"I KNEW SOME GREAT MUSICAL
 SHIT WAS ABOUT TO GO DOWN; I COULD
FEEL IT IN MY BONES. AND IT HAPPENED.
IT WENT ALL THE WAY DOWN."

PART OF MILES'S GENIUS WAS KNOWING HOW TO PUT MUSICIANS TOGETHER, AND THIS VERY WELL MAY HAVE BEEN HIS MOST BRILLIANT CONCEPTION. CENTRAL TO THE SEXTET'S SUCCESS WOULD BE CANNONBALL'S BLUES-BASED SOUND SET AGAINST TRANE'S UNIQUE, HIGH ENERGY APPROACH TO HARMONY AND FORM. THE RESULT WAS SHEER ALCHEMY — A NEW KIND OF SOUND — BIG BANG CREATIONS OF EXPANDING GALAXIES OF SOUND.

MILES DESCRIBED IT BEST IN HIS AUTOBIOGRAPHY:

"TRANE WOULD PLAY SOME WEIRD, GREAT SHIT, AND CANNONBALL WOULD TAKE IT IN THE OTHER DIRECTION, AND I WOULD PUT MY SOUND RIGHT DOWN THE MIDDLE OR FLOAT OVER IT...MIGHT PLAY REAL FAST, OR BUZZZZZ....THIS WOULD TAKE TRANE SOMEPLACE ELSE... AND THEN PAUL'S ANCHORING ALL THIS CREATIVE TENSION BETWEEN THE HORNS, AND RED'S LAYING  *DOWN HIS LIGHT, HIP SHIT, AND PHILLY JOE PUSHING EVERYTHING WITH ...THEM HIP-DE-DIP, SLICK RIM SHOTS ...,THEM 'PHILLY LICKS.' MAN, THAT WAS TOO HIP AND BAD."*

THE WHOLE SCENE WAS *TOO HIP AND BAD* AND IT WAS CRYSTALIZED ON THE NEW SEXTET'S FIRST RECORDING WHICH, APTLY ENOUGH, WAS CALLED *MILESTONES.*

73

MILESTONES, THE TITLE CUT, AND THELONIOUS MONK'S STRAIGHT, NO CHASER, SHARE HONORS AS THE MOST IMPORTANT AND MEMORABLE CUTS ON THE ALBUM. EACH TUNE IS SET UP BY CANNONBALL'S BIG, ROUND, ROLLING SOUND (WITH A LITTLE TOUCH OF TRANE), FOLLOWED BY MILES'S SPARE MUSINGS WITH PHILLY JOE LIGHTING FLASH FIRES BENEATH THEM, LEAVING COLTRANE TO BURST INTO BREATHLESS, BRILLIANT, BOUNDLESS, SCREAMING IMPROVISATIONS. THOUGH BOTH CUTS ARE GENUINE MASTERPIECES, IT WAS MILESTONES THAT HERALDED ONE OF THE MOST IMPORTANT STRUCTURAL INNOVATIONS IN JAZZDOM: MODAL JAZZ. ♪

Blue Note

Jazz scholar James Lincoln Collier defines a mode as *"a collection of notes a — scale, if you will — through which the composer or improvisor is free to wander as he wishes."* Miles, in an interview with Nat Hentoff, continues the thought, *"When you go this way, you can go on forever. You don't have to worry about changes and you can do more with the line. It becomes a challenge to see how melodically inventive you are. When you're based on chords, you know at the end of 32 bars that the chords run out and there's nothing to do but repeat what you've just done — with variations."* Miles went on to say that modal music represented a movement *"away from the conventional string of chords, and a return to emphasis on melodic rather than harmonic variation. There will be fewer chords but infinite possibilities with what to do with them."*

BUT, WHILE MILESTONES INTRODUCED THE WORLD TO MODAL JAZZ INVENTIONS, THE SEXTET'S NEXT RECORDING DATE, KIND OF BLUE (1959), PRODUCED IT'S MOST MAGNIFICENT REALIZATION, AND ALSO ONE OF THE GREATEST JAZZ ALBUMS EVER CREATED.

THE SEXTET HAD UNDERGONE A FEW CHANGES BETWEEN
MILESTONES AND *KIND OF BLUE*. JIMMY COBB ASSUMED THE
DRUMMER'S SPOT PARTLY BECAUSE PHILLY JOE'S CONTINUED
DRUG USE AND UNRELIABILITY RANKLED MILES. AND AFTER
SOME CREATIVE DISAGREEMENTS BETWEEN THE BOSS AND
THE PIANO PLAYER, RED GARLAND WALKED. HE WAS
REPLACED BY BILL EVANS WHOSE OWN MODAL MUSINGS WERE
IN KEEPING WITH MILES'S VISION, AND BY WYNTON KELLY, WHO
WAS ON TIME AS WELL.

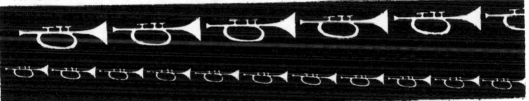

KIND OF BLUE IS THE STUFF OF LEGEND. MILES ENTERED THE
STUDIO WITH MUSICAL SKETCHES BORN ONLY HOURS BEFORE.
THE BAND DID NOT REHEARSE. THEY IMPROVISED FROM THE
BAREST OF OUTLINES. THE FIRST TAKES WERE MASTER TAKES,
AND THE MASTER TAKES WERE MASTERPIECES. PLAIN AND
SIMPLE. THEY WERE AS SPONTANEOUS AS AN ACT OF NATURE,
AS BEAUTIFUL AS A CONFLUENCE OF RIVERS, AND AS SOUL-
BLUESY AS THOSE DISTANT ARKANSAS NIGHTS.

BUT, AS THE MILES DAVIS SEXTET STOOD AT THE TOP OF THE
WORLD OF JAZZ, THE GOOD TIMES WERE NOT TO LAST.
CANNONBALL WAS DETERMINED TO HOOK UP WITH BROTHER
NAT ADDERLY AND SWING IN A FAMILY GROOVE. COLTRANE
WAS ITCHING TO LEAVE AS WELL, AS HIS BURGEONING MUSI-
CAL IDEAS WERE GROWING BEYOND THE POINT OF
CONTAINMENT. ♪

MILESTONES 1959

• CLEOTA DAVIS IS DIAGNOSED AS HAVING CANCER. • MILES IS BEATEN UP AND ARRESTED BY A WHITE POLICE OFFICER FOR LOITERING OUTSIDE BIRDLAND WHERE, AS THE OFFICER KNOWS, MILES'S COMBO IS HEADLINING. • SHORTLY AFTER THE KIND OF BLUE SESSIONS, TRANE GOES INTO THE STUDIO AND RECORDS *GIANT STEPS* FOR ATLANTIC RECORDS. • AFTER MUCH TALK, CANNONBALL FINALLY LEAVES THE BAND IN SEPTEMBER. • LATE IN THE YEAR MILES AND GIL EVANS, (WITH WHOM HE'D PRODUCED *MILES AHEAD* IN 1957 AND *PORGY AND BESS* IN 1958) START WORK ON THEIR MOST TRIUMPHANT COLLABORATION, *SKETCHES OF SPAIN.*

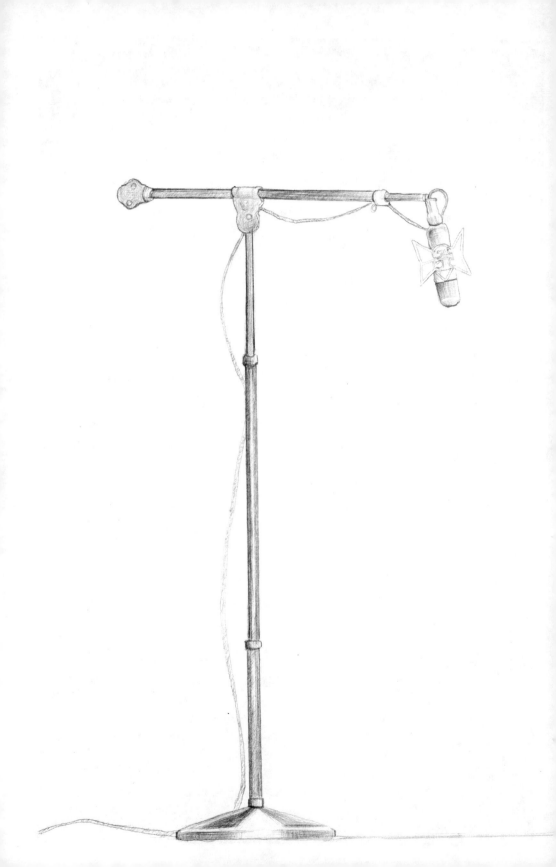

Blue Note

...a lonely Andalusian voice — an appropriate role for jazz's most *"...subtle delineator of loneliness,"* the man with the mystique. In the late 1950's the phrase *"The Miles Davis Mystique"* was coined. It became a kind of shorthand acknowledgement of the enigma without presuming to be able to explain him. Why *the enigma?* Here was a Negro — not an African-American, not an *Afro*-American, not even a Black man, but a *1950's Negro* — with a passion for beautiful women, clothes, and cars. A Negro who refused to be exploited economically or otherwise, by the white owners of the music. (One club owner made the mistake of insisting that Miles and the combo wear uniforms, whereupon Miles pulled a rack of clothing onto the stage and announced to the audience that the boss *"...wanted to see uniforms onstage so here they are. If that's what you came for...that's what you got. Now we're going to leave so you can enjoy these uniforms."*) A Negro who showed his contempt for the status quo (and perhaps for women as well) by referring to the secretaries at Columbia as *"white bitches."* A Negro who defied the police. A Negro who after winning another *Down Beat* poll, responded to their request that he take out a *"thank you"* ad with a simple *"fuck you."* Miles was arrogant, angry, and fierce. When Elaine Lorillard, co-organizer of the 1955 Newport Jazz Festival introduced him at a party as *"...the boy who played so beautifully,"* Miles snapped, *"Fuck you, an ain't no fucking boy! My name is Miles Davis, and you'd better remember that if you ever want to talk to me."* He seemed to have no regard for his audience — he was an entertainer as well as an artist, yet he refused to play the role of the entertainer — No Louis Armstrong pearly white displays, no Dizzy comic dizziness. (His was an extreme reaction, perhaps, against the happy barrelhouse darky images of his youth.) He never announced his tunes — the music spoke for itself. He was perceived to be anti-white, anti-social, anti-establishment. He was fiercely critical of his fellow musicians. He was intensely private. Yet, his music was full of warmth, and lyric beauty. He endured the scorn of an increasingly self-aware Black community because he had whites in his band. Nat Hentoff wrote that Miles was *"...sardonic, impatient with pretentiousness and cant, but also highly intelligent, acutely sensitive to and concerned with audience reactions, and in his personal relationships, inordinately helpful, generous,.... He is also shy."* So here we have the shy bon vivant, the evil creator of sublime beauty, the racist integrator, the self-absorbed altruist, the feline salty dog, the Man with the Horn, the Evil Genius. In 1964 Dizzy Gillespie announced his bid for the U.S. presidency in *Down Beat* magazine. When asked about his prospective appointees his friend Miles was among them. *"Head of the CIA." "Why?" "O-o-oh, honey, you know his schtick. He's ready for that position. He'd know what to do in that position."*

IN 1960 MILES'S WORLD
BECAME A RADICALLY DIFFER-
ENT PLACE. ON THE SURFACE
THINGS WERE COOL ENOUGH.
MILES WAS COMMANDING
$4,000 A GIG, AND CRUISIN' IN
A FERRARI. HE HAD EVEN
APPEARED AS A G.Q.-CLEAN
FASHION PLATE IN A MEN'S
FASHION MAGAZINE. BUT,
BELOW THE SURFACE, THINGS
WERE FALLING APART.

THE BOSS COMBO, WITH THE
DEPARTURE OF JOHN
COLTRANE, WAS BOSS NO
MORE. AND FOLLOWING
SKETCHES OF SPAIN MILES
AND GIL EVANS HAD NO DESIRE
TO RECORD TOGETHER FOR
SOME TIME TO COME. YET
MILES STILL HAD OBLIGATIONS
TO MEET AND DATES TO PER-
FORM. OVER TIME HE WOULD
ENLIST THE SERVICES OF AN
ARRAY OF VERY GIFTED MUSI-
CIANS, INCLUDING SAXOPHON-
ISTS SONNY STITT, HANK MOB-
LEY, AND GEORGE COLEMAN.
BUT, CLEARLY, THE ALCHEMY
WAS GONE. BASER METALS
REMAINED BASER METALS,
AND THE UNIVERSE WENT
UNALTERED, OR AT LEAST
UNALTERED BY MILES.....

IN FACT, THE UNIVERSE WAS CHANGING. THE IMPETUS BEHIND THIS CHANGE WAS NOT MILES DAVIS, BUT A SAXOPHONIST BY THE NAME OF ORNETTE COLEMAN. THE THE CHANGE TOOK A FORM CALLED *FREE JAZZ.*

Blue Note

In spite of Ozzie and Harriet's delightfully antiseptic vision of America in the 1950's, for many Americans revolution was in the air. *"Freedom now"* was the clarion call for those whose dreams had been too long deferred. Indeed, *"Blacks... felt a commitment to revolution. If freedom was good,"* describes James Lincoln Collier in *The Making of Jazz,* *" then the musician ought to liberate himself from the tyranny of bar lines, chord progressions, regular tempos, and even the pitches of the tempered scale."* The resulting free jazz was music that was essentially modal but filled with *"jagged phrasing, off-pitch honks and grunts, and... broken fragments of melody in what seemed to be random fashion."* By 1960 Coleman introduced an approach called *"harmonic unison"* which, ironically, was a dissonant sounding ensemble free association.

WHEN COLEMAN FIRST HIT THE NEW YORK JAZZ SCENE IN 1959, AS HE PUT IT, *"ALL HELL BROKE LOOSE."* MANY CRITICS ECHOED THE MOOD. MARTIN WILLIAMS WROTE, *"I BELIEVE THAT WHAT ORNETTE IS PLAYING WILL AFFECT THE WHOLE CHARACTER OF JAZZ MUSIC PROFOUNDLY AND PERVASIVELY."* JOHN LEWIS, PIANIST FOR THE MODERN JAZZ QUARTET STATED THAT *"ORNETTE COLEMAN IS DOING THE ONLY REALLY NEW THING IN JAZZ SINCE THE INNOVATIONS IN THE MID 40'S OF DIZZY GILLESPIE AND CHARLIE PARKER, AND THOSE OF THELONIOUS MONK."*

BUT
WHILE JOHN
LEWIS WAS AN
ENTHUSIASTIC
ADVOCATE OF
JAZZ'S NEW AVANT
GARDE, WILLIAMS
POINTS OUT THAT
MANY JAZZ MUSICIANS
WERE AFRAID THAT FREE
JAZZ WOULD RENDER
THEIR MUSIC OBSO-
LETE. MANY MUSI-
CIANS WERE CRITI-
CAL OF IT FOR THAT
REASON.

ONE OF ORNETTE COLEMAN'S MOST OUTSPOKEN CRITICS WAS MILES DEWEY DAVIS. ALTHOUGH IT'S DIFFICULT TO SAY THAT MILES WAS MOTIVATED BY A FEAR OF BECOMING OUTDATED, HIS "REACTIONARY" RESPONSE TO THE NEW MUSIC EFFECTIVELY DID JUST THAT.

"HELL, JUST LISTEN TO WHAT HE WRITES AND HOW HE PLAYS IT. IF YOU'RE TALKING PSYCHOLOGICALLY, THE MAN IS ALL SCREWED UP INSIDE."

MILES'S EXPLANATION OF THE NEW MUSIC'S CRITICAL SUCCESS WAS ALSO CHARACTERISTICALLY BLUNT:

"THEY WANT TO BE HIP.... WHITE PEOPLE ARE ESPECIALLY LIKE THAT, PARTICULARLY WHEN A BLACK PERSON IS DOING SOMETHING THEY DON'T UNDERSTAND."

THAT BEING SAID, MILES, NOW NEWLY OLD-FASHIONED, WAS QUICKLY CAST TO THE OUTSKIRTS OF HIP, AND THERE HE STAYED UNTIL 1963.

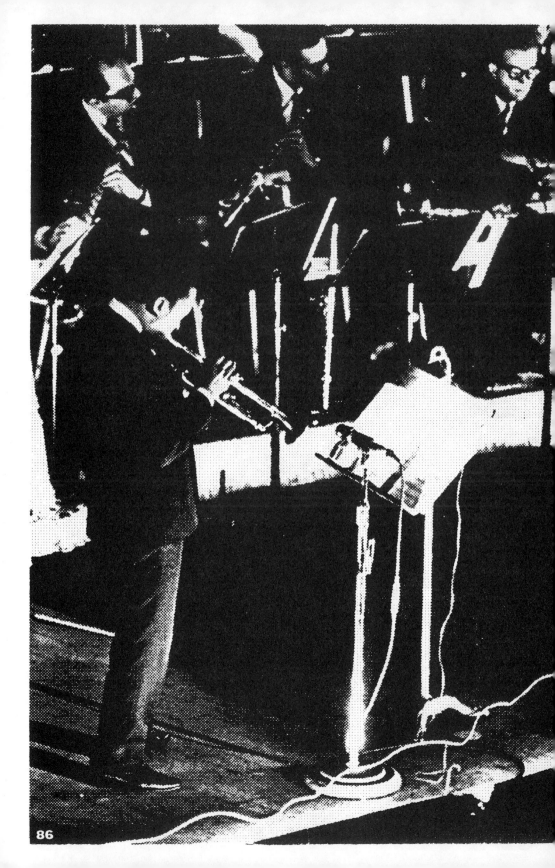

MILESTONES 1960 - 1962

• MILES MARRIES FRANCES TAYLOR (SEE APPENDIX A). • IN 1962 MILES'S FATHER, DOC DAVIS, DIES. • MILES, WHILE WORKING ON A CHRISTMAS ALBUM (WHICH HE IMMEDIATELY CHOSE TO FORGET), GOT A TASTE OF WAYNE SHORTER'S INTENSE *TRANE-ESQUE* GROOVE.

FOR THREE YEARS THE PRINCE OF DARKNESS MARKED TIME. BUT, IN 1963-4, HE PUT TOGETHER A NEW QUINTET WITH YOUNGER BLOODS, AND *SOMETHING HAPPENED.* MILES'S HORN, IN ALL ITS LYRIC RICHNESS COULD BE HEARD ANEW. IRONICALLY, IT HAD BEEN ALTERED BY THE FREE JAZZ SENSIBILITIES OF THE YOUNGER WARRIORS. ARMED WITH A PASSION FOR THE FREEDOM OF THE *MOMENT,* THEY CRAFTED EXQUISITE TROJAN HORSE MELODIES — TIMELESS, HYPNOTIC, EMBRACEABLE MELODIES — AND LAUNCHED CROSS-RHYTHMIC, FLUX-TIME, CRAZY-FIRE, HARD SWINGIN' ATTACKS ON THE OLD MUSICAL ORDER. NOW THE EXILED PRINCE, YOUNG WARRIORS AT HIS FLANKS, STOOD ON THE BRINK OF RE-TAKING THE THRONE. THE WARRIORS WERE FOUR.

Miles at Carnegie Hall, May 19, 1961.

A TIME-SAVVY BASSIST NAMED RON CARTER.

"...RON WAS A MOTHERFUCKER OF A BASS PLAYER."

A FRESH-FACED PIANIST NAMED HERBIE HANCOCK.

"...NICE TOUCH, KID." (HIGH PRAISE TO A PIANO PLAYER COMING FROM MILES!)

AN IRREPRESSIBLE YOUNG HORNBLOWER NAMED WAYNE SHORTER.

"WAYNE WAS THE ONLY PERSON THAT I KNEW THEN WHO WROTE SOMETHING LIKE THE WAY BIRD WROTE, THE ONLY ONE."

AND A 17 YEAR-OLD WHIZ-KID DRUMMER NAMED TONY WILLIAMS.

"TONY... JUST BLEW MY FUCKING MIND HE WAS SO BAD.... MAN JUST HEARING THAT LITTLE MOTHERFUCKER MADE ME EXCITED ALL OVER AGAIN."

AND WITH THEIR AID, THE THRONE WAS SOON HIS AGAIN.

THE
LEGENDARY COMBO
OF THE 1950'S WAS
ONE OF THE
GREATEST IN THE
HISTORY OF THE
MUSIC. BUT
WHEN THE
NEW

COMBO FINALLY
CAME TOGETHER,
"MILES EMBARKED ON
A NEW ERA OF DIS-
COVERY THAT
RIVALED HIS 1955-9
PERIOD." (HARVEY
PEKAR, CODA)

AND THIS PERIOD
DID HUM. OVER
THE NEXT FOUR
YEARS MILES
WOULD RELEASE
SIX STUDIO
RECORDINGS THAT,
TO MANY, REPRE-
SENT THE FINEST
MUSIC HE EVER PRO-
DUCED.

IN THE NEW MILES DAVIS QUINTET, MILES BROUGHT
MILES: THE ELDER, THE INSPIRATION, THE SAGE, THE
GRIOT. WAYNE BROUGHT THE COMPOSITIONS, THE
CONCEPTS, THE IDEAS, MAN, THOSE *IDEAS*. HERBIE
BROUGHT A KIND OF FREE FORM PUNCTUATION AND,
ALONG WITH THE GRAND UNIFYING QUALITY OF RON'S
BASS PLAYING, THE TWO ANCHORED THE MUSIC.

Blue Note

During the Miles Davis Quintet years, Wayne Shorter recorded a number of albums as a leader on the Blue Note label. One such album, *Adam's Apple* featured Wayne's composition, *Footprints*, which a couple months later was recorded by the Miles Davis Quintet on *Miles Smiles*. To get a sense of how music was transformed within the milieu of the Miles Davis Quintet, give both a careful listen, and, in the author's opinion, you'll hear the difference between the merely beautiful and the clearly transcendent.

BUT IT WAS THE BAND'S DRUMMER, TONY WILLIAMS, WHO BROUGHT BOUNDLESS ENTHUSIASM AS WELL AS SPEED, FIRE, AND A SUBTLE MASTERY OF TIME TO THE BAND. HE DROVE THE BAND FOR THE NEXT FOUR YEARS. BETWEEN TONY AND RON, THE RHYTHMS WERE EVER CROSSED, NEVER STILL. THE HORNMEN WERE PUSHED TO NEW LEVELS, AND GROOVED TO A DIFFERENT PULSE, BECAUSE THEY HAD TO, *HAD TO*. *PARTICULARLY MILES.*

"EVERY NIGHT HERBIE, TONY, AND RON WOULD...COME BACK AND PLAY SOMETHING DIFFERENT. AND EVERY NIGHT I WOULD HAVE TO REACT."

MILES REACTED BEAUTIFULLY, AND MASTERPIECES WERE BORN, LIKE *E.S.P.* (E.S.P.), *FOOTPRINTS* AND *CIRCLE* (MILES SMILES), AND *NEFERTITI* (NEFERTITI).

MILESTONES 1964-7

• IN 1964 MILES'S MOTHER, CLEOTA, DIES, AND MILES FAILS TO ATTEND HER FUNERAL, OPTING INSTEAD TO GO HOME AND CRY *"LIKE A MOTHERFUCKER ALL NIGHT."* • COMPLICATIONS DUE TO SICKLE CELL ANEMIA CAUSE MILES INCREASING DISCOMFORT. • MILES AND FRANCES THROW A STAR-STUDDED PARTY FOR BOBBY KENNEDY. • IN APRIL 1965 MILES RECEIVES A HIP OPERATION, AND RECUPERATES WHILE WATCHING THE WATTS RIOTS ON TV. • IN EARLY 1966 MILES IS CONFINED TO BED DUE TO A LIVER INFECTION. • IN THAT SAME YEAR MILES MEETS CICELY TYSON FOR THE FIRST TIME. • ON JULY 17, 1967, JOHN COLTRANE, NOW THE VOICE OF REVOLUTION FOR AFRICAN- AMERICAN INTELLECTUALS OF THE DAY, DIES.

IN 1968 A CERTAIN RESTLESSNESS COULD BE FELT IN THE BAND AS SIDEMEN FELT THE NEED TO BECOME LEADERS, AND THE QUINTET'S LAST ALBUM, *FILLES DE KILIMANJARO* (1968) MARKED THE COMBO'S TRANSITIONAL MOOD. IT INTRODUCED CHICK COREA ON PIANO AND DAVE HOLLAND ON BASS. IT INTRODUCED THE ELECTRIC PIANO (INSPIRED BY CANNONBALL'S PIANIST JOE ZAWINAL) INTO MILES ACOUSTIC WORLD. IT MARKED THE BEGINNING OF WHAT WAS SOON TO BECOME A MASSIVE RIFT BETWEEN THE LOVERS OF THE ELECTRIC AND THE PRE-ELECTRIC MILES. MOREOVER, IT REFLECTED HOW THE CHANGING TIMES WERE CHANGING MILES.

IN 1968 THE COUNTRY WAS ON FIRE. AFTER GLIMPSING THE PROMISED LAND, MARTIN LUTHER KING, JR., WAS ASSASSINATED HUEY NEWTON AND BOBBY SEALE FOUNDED THE *BLACK PANTHERS* TO PROTECT OAKLAND'S AFRICAN-AMERICAN COMMUNITY FROM POLICE ABUSE; BOBBY KENNEDY WAS GUNNED DOWN AND IN VIETNAM THE WAR RAGED ON.

IN THE MUSIC OF THE DAY A REBELLIOUS HALF OF A NATION FOUND ITS VOICE. BUT IT WAS NOT THE VOICE OF JAZZ. IT WAS THE VOICE OF ROCK. IT WAS THE VOICE THAT SPOKE TO YOUTH AND IT BECAME THE VOICE WITH WHICH MILES YEARNED TO SPEAK.

FOUR YEARS EARLIER WHEN THE CRY WENT UP THAT JAZZ WAS DEAD, AND JAZZMEN RETREATED EN MASSE TO PARIS AND MOROCCO, MILES VOWED NEVER TO LET HIS VOICE DIE WITH THE MUSIC, NEVER TO BECOME A LIVING RELIC. SO, IF JAZZ WAS FATED TO BECOME AMERICA'S CLASSICAL MUSIC AND PLACED IN A MUSEUM TO BE STUDIED AND REVERED, IT WOULD DO SO WITHOUT MILES. (PERHAPS MILES NEEDED TO BE ALWAYS CURRENT DUE, PART, TO THE SEVERE POPULAR AND CRITICAL BACKLASH HE EXPERIENCED IN THE ORNETTE COLEMAN DAYS.)

MILES ENTERED 1968 MARRIED TO FRANCES AND WAS SPENDING TIME WITH CICELY TYSON. BUT, BY SEPTEMBER PAPA MILES, NOW 42, HAD A BRAND NEW SQUEEZE — BETTY MABRY, 23 YEARS-OLD, MOD, AND BEAUTIFUL. BETTY INTRODUCED MILES TO JIMI HENDRIX. SHE ALSO BROUGHT MILES'S LOOK UP TO DATE — THE PRINCE OF DARKNESS WAS NOW MOD TOO, DONNING HIS ANIMAL SKIN ROBES, STUDDED LEATHER ACCESSORIES, ELEPHANT BELLS, AND STACKS.

AS FOR THE *MUSIC*, BETTY HELPED TUNE MILES'S EAR TO A GROOVY GROOVE, TO THE SOUND OF HENDRIX AND SLY STONE. AS THESE SOUNDS SEEPED INTO MILES'S MUSICAL IMAGINATION, THE MUSIC IN HIS HEAD STARTED TO CHANGE. IN 1969 MILES RECORDED THE LANDMARK FUSION ALBUM *BITCHES BREW*, COMPLETE WITH ELECTRIC PIANO, ELECTRIC TRUMPET, ELECTRIC BASS, ELECTRIC GUITAR, PERCUSSIONS AND BONGOS.♪

Blue Note

It was Charles Lloyd and not Miles Davis who *"created"* fusion. In 1967- 8 Lloyd began to play a kind of jazz-rock, and his quartet soon became known as the *"first psychedelic jazz group."* It is generally agreed, however, that Lloyd's fusion had less to do with vision than with circumstance. His sidemen, pianist Keith Jarrett and drummer Jack DeJohnette were young and in touch with the 60's pop scene. But, when it came to layin' down that groovy rap, Lloyd was right on time. Dig: *"I play love vibrations. Love totality — like bringing everyone together in a joyous dance."* Rap on, brother, rap on.

BITCHES BREW WAS A SWIRL OF ROCK-JAZZ IMPROVISATIONS AND WAS MILES'S BEST-SELLING ALBUM TO DATE. IT SOLD OVER 400,000 LP'S IN ITS FIRST YEAR, MORE THAN ANY OTHER JAZZ ALBUM IN HISTORY. MOREOVER, IT PLACED MILES EXACTLY WHERE HE WANTED TO BE — IN THE WORLD OF THE LIVING AND IN THE FOREFRONT OF THE NEW SOUND.

MILES WAS NOW GETTING GIGS AT PLACES LIKE THE FILMORE WEST, THE PREMIER ROCK EMPORIUM OF THE DAY, AND OPENING FOR GROUPS LIKE THE GRATEFUL DEAD.

BUT, FOR ALL OF MILES'S POPULAR SUCCESS, HIS NEW MUSIC MET WITH RESISTANCE FROM THE JAZZ MAINSTREAM. CHARGES OF SELLING OUT WERE LEVELED, PARTICULARLY WHEN IT BECAME CLEAR THAT MILES WAS NOT TURNING BACK.

OF COURSE THE MONEY DIDN'T *HURT*....

"[ROCK MUSICIANS] WERE POPULAR AND SOLD A LOT OF RECORDS.... SO I FIGURED IF THEY COULD DO IT — REACH ALL THOSE PEOPLE AND SELL ALL THOSE RECORDS WITHOUT REALLY KNOWING WHAT THEY WERE DOING — THEN I COULD DO IT TOO, ONLY BETTER."

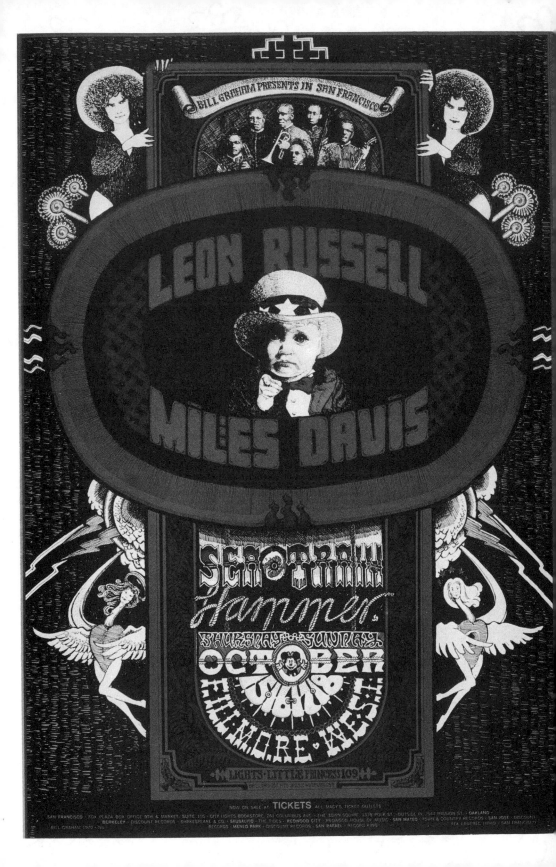

...AND WHILE THAT *DOES* SOUND A *LITTLE* LIKE A SELL OUT, GUITARIST JOHN SCOFIELD, STATES THAT MILES *"WANTED PEOPLE TO COME TO HIS GIGS AND DIG IT, YOU KNOW? HE DIDN'T WANT TO BE AN ESOTERIC JAZZ LEGEND. HE COULD MAKE A BELIEVER OUT OF A NONJAZZ PERSON WITH THE BEAUTY OF HIS SOUND AND HIS RHYTHM AND HIS NOTES. THAT'S PRETTY HEAVY."* (MUSICIAN MAGAZINE, DEC 1991.)

MILESTONES 1969-70

• **AFTER A GIG AT BROOKLYN'S BLUE CORONET CLUB, MILES IS SHOT, ALLEGEDLY BECAUSE SOME BLACK PROMOTERS OBJECTED TO WHITE PROMOTERS BOOKING HIS GIGS. • IN THE FALL OF '69 WAYNE SHORTER LEAVES, AND NOW, WITH TONY AND HERBIE ALREADY GONE, MILES BREAKS UP THE BAND. • IN AUGUST MILES PLAYS THE ISLE OF WIGHT CON-CERT IN ENGLAND ALONG WITH HENDRIX AND OTHER ROCKERS. SHORTLY AFTER THE CONCERT, HENDRIX DIES IN LONDON. • MILES STARTS TO USE A *"WAH-WAH"* PEDAL ON HIS TRUMPET TO *"GET CLOSER TO THAT VOICE JIMI HAD WHEN HE USED A WAH-WAH ON HIS GUITAR."***

OVER THE NEXT FIVE YEARS, MILES WOULD TAKE THE MUSIC INTO A DEEP FUNK GROOVE, WHICH CRITIC GREG TATE WOULD CALL AN "ACID FUNK" JAZZ GROOVE. YET MILES DEFIED THE CRITICS TO CATEGORIZE HIM, INSISTING THAT HE PLAYED WHAT THE DAY RECOMMENDED. WHAT THE DAY NOW RECOMMENDED WAS THAT THE MUSIC TURN AWAY FROM YOUNG WHITE AUDIENCES AND SPEAK TO YOUNG BLACK AMERICA. THE FOLLOWING IS A CBS RECORDS AD BLURB ACCOMPANYING THE RELEASE OF *ON THE CORNER* (1972). *"TAKE A WALK DOWN A CITY STREET WITH MILES DAVIS AND LISTEN TO THE LANGUAGE OF THE PEOPLE ON THE SIDEWALK. LISTEN TO MUSIC THAT CAPTURES THE JOY, THE PAIN, THE BEAUTY OF PEOPLE WHO LIVE ON 'THE BLOCK,' LISTEN TO ONE OF THE MOST BEAUTIFUL PLACES IN THE WORLD."*

NOT ONLY DID MILES PLAY WHAT THE DAY RECOMMENDED, BUT HE PLAYED WITH *WHOM* THE DAY RECOMMENDED. DURING THESE YEARS, HE WOULD EMPLOY THE TALENTS OF A SCORE OF MUSICIANS, INCLUDING A CORE OF 37 WHO BECAME KNOWN AS *"MILES'S STOCK COMPANY PLAYERS."*

AT ITS BEST THE MUSIC WAS LIKE A *"...A DENSE ELECTRONIC RAIN FOREST.... ECHOING, REVERBERATING, ELECTRONICALLY SHAPED NOTES AND PHRASES FORM THE STRANGE BEAUTIFUL FOLIAGE AND STRONG LIFE RHYTHMS OF DAVIS'S MUSICAL WORLD."* (GENE WILLIAMS, WASHINGTON POST)

YET, IN SPITE OF SUCH ENCHANTING DESCRIPTIONS, AND MILES'S OWN BELIEF THAT 1969-75 WAS FOR HIM A "GREAT CREATIVE PERIOD," THINGS BEGAN TO SLIP. SOMETHING WAS GETTING IN THE WAY OF THE MUSIC. PERHAPS IT WAS THE COCAINE AND THE DOWNERS, AND THE VOICES IN HIS HEAD — THOSE DAMN TINY PEOPLE SHOUTING AT HIM FROM INSIDE RADIATORS, UNDER RUGS AND SOFAS.. PERHAPS IT WAS THE WOMEN, ALL THOSE WOMEN — THE ONES IN THE POLAROIDS *"FREAKING OUT ON THEMSELVES"* FOR MILES'S AMUSEMENT AND DRIVING HIM TO DISTRACTION. PERHAPS IT WAS THE HIP PAIN, THE LIVER PAIN, THE THROAT NODES AND BURSITIS PAIN, THE I'VE GOT SICKLE-CELL, DIABETES, AND I'M STILL LIVIN' FAST PAIN. THAT 47 YEARS OLD AND GOIN' ON 19 PAIN. PERHAPS IT WAS THE HERBIE HANCOCK'S *"HEADHUNTERS"* FUSION ALBUM IS SELLIN' LIKE A MOTHERFUCKER IN THE COMMUNITY WHILE MY SHIT'S FALLIN FLAT AND NOW I'M AN OPENING ACT FOR MY EX-SIDEMAN *BLUES* KIND OF PAIN.

WHATEVER IT WAS, IT HAD PEOPLE TALKING ABOUT AN "EMPEROR'S NEW CLOTHES" THING HAPPENING WITH THE MUSIC. IT HAD ONCE FAITHFUL AUDIENCES BOOING. IT HAD ALBUM PRODUCTION DROPPING OFF. AND IT HAD MILES DAVIS, FOR THE FIRST TIME IN HIS CAREER, THINKING ABOUT RETIRING. FINALLY, IN THE SUMMER OF 1975, WHEN THE MUSIC WAS ENOUGH, MILES, THE THINNING SHADOWMAN, FADED FROM THE SCENE.

"I QUIT PRIMARILY BECAUSE OF HEALTH REASONS, BUT ALSO BECAUSE I WAS SPIRITUALLY TIRED.... I FELT ARTISTICALLY DRAINED, TIRED. I DIDN'T HAVE ANYTHING ELSE TO SAY MUSICALLY."

1975-80 SAW MILES RETREAT INTO A DARK WORLD DEVOID OF MUSIC — *DEVOID OF MUSIC.*

"MOSTLY DURING THOSE FOUR OR FIVE YEARS THAT I WAS OUT OF MUSIC, I JUST TOOK A LOT OF COCAINE.... AND FUCKED ALL THE WOMEN I COULD GET INTO MY HOUSE."

AND SO IT WENT

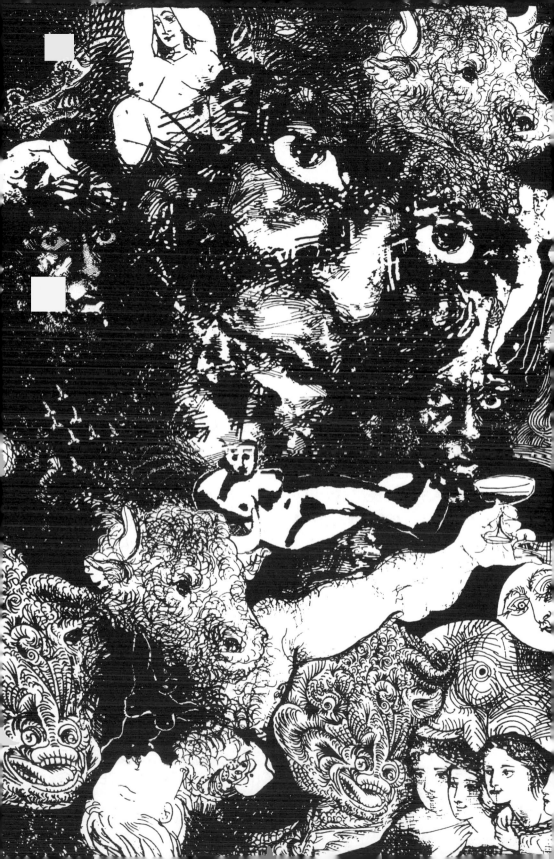

MILES EVENTUALLY GREW BORED WITH HIS DARK AND BIZARRE, MUSICLESS LIFE. SO, WITH THE ENCOURAGEMENT OF THE FEW PEOPLE HE LET NEAR HIM, LIKE GEORGE BUTLER, DIZZY GILLESPIE, AND CICELY TYSON (SHE WEANED HIM OFF THE BOOZE, FLOOZIES, COKE AND PILLS), MILES DAVIS – BLACK PHOENIX – ROSE AGAIN. AND FIVE YEARS OF THE MOST INSANE DEBAUCHERY FINALLY CAME TO AN END.

IN 1980 THE HORN ONCE AGAIN TOUCHED HIS LIPS, AND IN 1981 THE SHADOWMAN STEPPED INTO THE PUBLIC LIGHT. THE MAN WITH THE HORN WAS BACK, BUT *THE MUSIC*... WELL THAT WAS SOMETHING ELSE. THAT WOULD TAKE TIME.

MILES'S COMEBACK CONCERTS WERE THE MOST HIGHLY PUBLICIZED SPECTACLES IN THE HISTORY OF JAZZ, AND WERE IMMEDIATE SELLOUTS. HIS PLAYING, HOWEVER, OFTEN LEFT THE EAGER CROWDS DISAPPOINTED. HIS HEALTH WAS STILL A PROBLEM, HIS CHOPS HAD SUFFERED DURING HIS LAYOFF. MOREOVER, HIS CONFIDENCE HAD SUFFERED, AND IRONICALLY, THE MAN WHO HAD *INVENTED* COOL WAS BEING CONSUMED BY THE JITTERS.

MEANWHILE, MILES'S FIRST *RECORDED* EFFORTS, WHILE SELLING WELL, WERE CLEARLY BELOW PAR. IN REVIEWING *WE WANT MILES* (1981), CRITIC FRANCIS DAVIS TO WROTE THAT *"...THE MILES WE WANT AND THE MILES WE'RE WILLING TO SETTLE FOR ARE OFTEN ENTIRELY DIFFERENT CREATURES."* TO BE FAIR, MILES *HAD* BEEN AWAY FROM THE MUSIC FOR FIVE YEARS. AND FUSION, SUCH AS HE LEFT IT IN THE MID-70'S HAD FALLEN OUT OF FAVOR, RENDERING MILES SLIGHTLY OUT OF STEP.

MILESTONES 1981-82

• MILES DOES EIGHT SHOWS IN JAPAN FOR WHICH HE RECEIVES $700,000. • ON THANKSGIVING MILES MARRIES LONG-TIME FRIEND AND LOVER CICELY TYSON — FIVE DAYS LATER HE HAS HIS FIRST AFFAIR. • LATER IN THE YEAR MILES SUFFERS A STROKE WHICH TEMPORILY PARALYZES HIS RIGHT HAND. BY 1982 HE IS UNDERWEIGHT AND RAPIDLY LOSING HIS HAIR. • WHILE ON A 1982 EUROPEAN TOUR HE EMBRACES HIS MOST ENDURING MISTRESS — THE VISUAL ARTS — AND HE BEGINS TO *DRAW.*

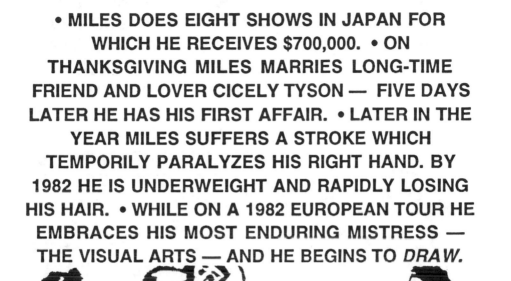

IN LATE 1982, HOWEVER, THINGS WERE COMING TOGETHER AGAIN. MILES WAS GETTING STRONGER AND HEALTHIER, AND LEE JESKE REPORTED THAT MILES WAS A NEW MAN ON STAGE, *"MUGGING TO THE AUDIENCE, TWICE STEPPING UP TO AN UNATTENDED MIKE PRETENDING TO BE ABOUT TO SING, GRINNING AND PRANCING."*

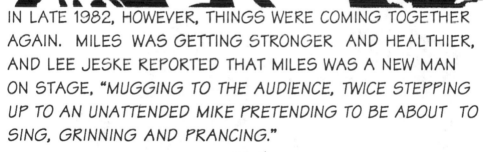

LATE THAT YEAR AND INTO THE NEXT, MILES WENT INTO THE STUDIO WITH HARD SWINGING DRUMMER AL FOSTER, BLUE NOTE BENDING GUITARIST MIKE STERN, AND THE MORE COSMO-HIP GUITARIST JOHN SCOFIELD AND TOGETHER THEY CREATED THE BLUES ORIENTED *STAR PEOPLE.* AS WITH HIS 1954 RECORDING OF *WALKIN',* MILES ONCE AGAIN FOUND HIMSELF TURNING TO THE BLUES TO RESURRECT THE MUSIC, AND THE MUSIC RESURRECTED MILES.

MILESTONES 1983-84

• MILES IS HONORED AT NEW YORK'S RADIO CITY MUSIC HALL IN NOVEMBER 1983 IN A CELEBRATION ENTITLED *"MILES AHEAD: A TRIBUTE TO AN AMERICAN MUSIC LEGEND."* AT THE CELEBRATION HE IS AWARDED AN HONORARY DEGREE IN MUSIC FROM FISK UNIVERSITY.

• IN NOVEMBER OF 1984, MILES RECEIVES THE SONNING MUSIC AWARD FOR LIFE-TIME ACHIEVEMENT, AN AWARD USUALLY RESERVED FOR CLASSICAL MUSICIANS.

MUCH OF THE MUSIC FROM THE MID 1980'S ON HAD A DECIDEDLY COMMERCIAL CHARACTER. FURTHERMORE, HIS APPROACH TO STUDIO RECORDING FOLLOWED CONVENTIONAL POP METHODS, THAT IS, THE MUSIC WAS RECORDED LAYER BY LAYER AND ENGINEERED INTO PLACE. YET MILES, WITH THE HELP OF MARCUS MILLER, CONTINUED TO WORK ON PROJECTS AND WITH THEM HIS POPULARITY GREW.

MILESTONES 1986
• MILES GUEST STARS ON AN EPISODE OF "MIAMI VICE" IN THE ROLE OF A PIMP. • HE ALSO DOES A HONDA COMMERCIAL, AND IN ONE FELL SWOOP, FINALLY BECOMES A UNIVERSALLY RECOGNIZED FIGURE.

IN 1986 MILES LEFT COLUMBIA RECORDS AND SIGNED ON WITH WARNER. HIS FIRST RECORD WITH WARNER, *TUTU* (NAMED AFTER THE ANTI-APARTHIED NOBEL LAUREATE, BISHOP DESMOND TUTU), WHILE PANNED BY THE CRITICS, WON MILES A GRAMMY AND SOLD WELL. MOREOVER, IT SECURED A PLACE FOR MILES AMONG YET ANOTHER GENERATION OF LISTENERS AND WAS SAMPLED BY DJ MARK THE 45 KING ON RAPPER QUEEN LATIFAH'S JAM, *ALL HAIL THE QUEEN.* (PRINCE, WHOM MILES HAD COME TO ADMIRE GREATLY AS A "LITTLE GENIUS" WROTE A PIECE FOR THE TUTU ALBUM, BUT IT WAS NOT INCLUDED ON THE ALBUM.)

MILESTONE 1988

• GIL EVANS, MILES'S LONG-TIME COLLABORATOR AND BEST FRIEND, DIES OF PERITONITIS.

JUST AS THE DAYS OF THE GREAT COMBOS WERE FOREVER GONE, BOWING TOO A KIND OF MODULAR APPROACH TO MUSIC MAKING, SO TOO WERE GONE THE DAYS OF MILES DAVIS LEADING THE MUSIC IN NEW DIRECTIONS. THIS VIEW WAS CONFIRMED BY MILES'S COVER OF CYNDI LAUPER'S *TIME AFTER TIME*. WHILE IT WAS A NICE VEHICLE FOR ONE OF THE FINEST BALLADEERS IN THE HISTORY OF JAZZ, IT WAS, AS FRANCIS DAVIS ARGUED, CYNDI LAUPER, NOT MILES DAVIS WHO SUPPLIED THE CONTEXT FOR THE MUSIC. JOHN SCOFIELD WOULD LATER SAY THAT MILES *"...DIDN'T WANT TO WORK HARD AT BEING AN INNOVATOR.... HE DIDN'T WANT TO SAY IT, BUT HE WANTED TO PLAY GOOD MUSIC AND MAKE GREAT MONEY."* FOR THE TIME THIS SEEMED TRUE.

STILL, MILES DAVIS WAS A CAULDRON OF CREATIVITY. ONE NEED ONLY TO LOOK TO HIS PAINTINGS TO FIND THE MUCH LAMENTED MISSING ARTISTIC SPARK.

WHETHER ONE FINDS MILES'S PAINTING AESTHETICALLY WORTHY OR NOT IS A MATTER OF TASTE. BUT, IT IS CLEAR THAT HIS CANVASES WERE FULL OF PASSION, ENERGY, AND SPONTANEITY, AND AT TIMES, SEEMED LIKE VISUAL MANIFESTATIONS OF *BITCHES BREW*.

MILES'S FIRST DRAWINGS WERE NAIVE FIGURES, BUT HE SOON DEVELOPED TASTE FOR COLOR AND COMPOSITIONAL EXPERIMENTATION. IN 1988, INSPIRED BY A MILANESE DESIGN MOVEMENT KNOWN AS *"MEMPHIS,"* MILES BEGAN TO PLAY WITH VIBRANTLY COLORED, CLASHING FORMS.

AFTER EXPLORING THE POSSIBILITIES OF *MEMPHIS*, MILES
WENT ON TO COLLABORATE WITH THE NEW YORK ARTIST
JO GELBARD. TOGETHER THEY LOOKED TO AFRICA FOR
INSPIRATION, AND SOON THE STUDIO THEY SHARED IN
MANHATTAN WAS TEEMING WITH AFRICAN IMAGERY.

(THE COVER ART OF MILES'S AMANDLA WAS CREATED BY MILES HIMSELF.) MILES WAS ALSO INFLUENCED BY THE LATE ARTIST JEAN-MICHEL BASQUIAT, AND THE SPANISH SURREALIST, JOAN MIRO. AS JO GELBARD PUT IT, "HE'S MORE INTERESTED IN THE IMAGINATION AND THE FREEDOM OF THE IMAGINATION.... HE LOVES LOOKING AT WORKS WHERE SOMETHING IS HIDDEN, WHERE YOU CAN CONSTANTLY FIND THINGS."

TO SUGGEST THAT MILES DIVERTED ENERGY AWAY FROM HIS MUSIC TO NOURISH HIS PAINTING MIGHT NOT BE CORRECT. YET, THE IMMEDIACY AND POWER OF HIS CANVASES COMMAND ATTENTION IN A WAY THAT HIS MUSIC, DURING THESE YEARS, DID ONLY SPORADICALLY. PERHAPS IT WAS BECAUSE HIS COURSE HERE WAS CLEAR AND INTUITIVE. CRITIC FRANCIS DAVIS WROTE OF MILES THE MUSICIAN: "POOR MILES. AS A THINKING MAN'S POP STAR, HE'S UNBANKABLE IN A MARKET THAT INCREASINGLY DEPENDS ON CONDITIONED REFLEX. AS A JAZZ PANJAN-DRUM, HE'S BEEN TRADING ON CREDIT FOR FAR TOO LONG." HIS PAINTING, UNLIKE HIS MUSIC, WAS NOT MARRED BY SUCH AMBIGUITIES.

FULL CIRCLE...

IN THE SUMMER OF 1991, MILES DAVIS, 65 YEAR-OLD STALWART, ONCE AGAIN PLACED HIMSELF AMONG THE HIPPEST MUSIC-MAKERS OF THE DAY — THE RAPPERS. ♪ THESE LATTER DAY KEEPERS OF THE BEBOP *SPIRIT* INTRIGUED MILES.

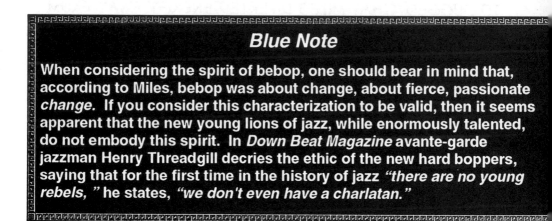

Blue Note

When considering the spirit of bebop, one should bear in mind that, according to Miles, bebop was about change, about fierce, passionate *change.* If you consider this characterization to be valid, then it seems apparent that the new young lions of jazz, while enormously talented, do not embody this spirit. In *Down Beat Magazine* avante-garde jazzman Henry Threadgill decries the ethic of the new hard boppers, saying that for the first time in the history of jazz *"there are no young rebels, "* he states, *"we don't even have a charlatan."*

IT WAS ONLY FITTING, THEREFORE, THAT MILES'S FINAL PROJECT WOULD BE DONE IN COLLABORATION WITH A YOUNG, BROOKLYN, NEW YORK–BASED RAPPER.

THE ALBUM IS *DOO BOP.* THE RAPPER IS EASY MO BEE. EASY, OF *RAPPING IS FUNDAMENTAL,* BROUGHT THE *DOO* FROM THE *DOO HOP* BORN OF A MARRIAGE OF *DOO WOP* AND *HIP HOP,* AND MILES, WELL MILES BROUGHT THE *BOP.*

AND SO TO A HIP-HOP BEAT, THE DARK PRINCE DEPARTED MUCH AS HE STARTED — LOOKING FOR A VOICE ON THE CUTTING EDGE. *WORD.*

L A S T   M I L E S . . .

ON SATURDAY, SEPTEMBER 28, 1991, MILES DEWEY DAVIS III DIED
AT ST. JOHN'S HOSPITAL AND HEALTH CENTER IN SANTA MONICA,
CALIFORNIA. THE CAUSES OF HIS DEATH WERE LISTED AS
PNEUMONIA, RESPIRATORY FAILURE, AND A STROKE.

TRUMPETER WALLACE RONEY HUNG OUT WITH MILES DURING THE
SUMMER OF 1991 AT THE MONTREAUX FESTIVAL. HE RECALLS THEIR
TIME TOGETHER. MILES *"...WAS TELLING ME EVERYTHING HE COULD
THINK OF ABOUT MUSIC, LIKE HE WAS TRYING TO CRAM 45 YEARS
OF MUSIC INTO THREE DAYS.....I DIDN'T THINK HE WAS GOING TO DIE,
BUT MAYBE HE DID. THINGS JUST SPILLED OUT; HE TALKED ABOUT
BIRD, DIZZY, MONK,.... HE KNEW HOW MUCH I LOVE HIM AND HE SAID
THAT'S COOL, BECAUSE THAT'S THE WAY HE LOVED DIZZY."*

WHEN LEGENDS PASS THERE OCCURS A REASSESSMENT OF THE
STATE OF THE ART BY THOSE LEFT BEHIND, AN ATTEMPT TO DEFINE
WHAT WAS JUST LOST. PIANIST KEITH JARRETT DEFINED THAT
LOSS THIS WAY: *"IT IS PURE INTENT. MILES WAS A RESONANCE
AND WHEN HE DIED, WE LOST THE RESONANCE. FOR ALL THE
YOUNG PLAYERS WHO WERE PLAYING IN THIS ROOM, THE
MATERIALS OF THE WALLS JUST CHANGED."* (MUSICIAN MAGAZINE,
DECEMBER 1991)

YES. AND COLTRANE SHOOK HIS HEAD AND FROWNED, *"I DON'T
KNOW, BUT HE THINKS HE'S MILES."*

WE ADMIT, PERHAPS GRUDGINGLY, THAT MILES DAVIS WAS NOT
GOD. AND JUDGING FROM SOME OF HIS LIFE DECISIONS, IT SEEMS
UNLIKELY THAT HE'D EARNED A PLACE IN GODLAND BUT, MILES
FIGURED THAT IN SPITE OF HIS FAULTS, THOSE IN HEAVEN
JUDGING HIS WORTHINESS OF A PLACE BESIDE GOD COULD ARRIVE
AT ONLY ONE DECISION, AND THEY WOULD BE COMPELLED TO SAY:
*"WELL HE'S THE ONLY ONE WHO CAN PLAY LIKE THAT; WE BETTER
LET HIM IN."*

Four, And More
For Miles Davis
by Quincy Troupe

1.

a carrier of incandescent dreams, this
blade-thin, shadowman, jagged by lightning
crystal silhouette
prowling over blues-stained pavements
his life, lean, he drapes himself, his music, across edges
his blood held tight, within
he takes risks in staccato flights

& clean as darkness & bright as lightning
he reverses moments, where the sound becomes two cat eyes
penetrating the midnight hours, of moon pearl faces
lacing broken, mirrored waters
mississippi mean, as this sun-drenched trumpet-man
is mean, holding dreams high on any wind, light

his voice walking on eggshells

2.

& time comes as the wrinkles
of your mother's skin shrinks inward
the spirit flying towards that compelling
voice, light, calling
since time began, on the flip-side of spirit, you
miles, shedding placentas at each stage of your
                            music
then go down river to explore
a new blues
the drum skin of young years wearing
long, the enigmatic search
of your music
changing. with every turning of the clock's hands
spinning your sound towards the diamond-point
in the river, lyrical, beyond edges
where light comes & goes

3.

O Silent Keeper of shadows
of these gutted, bloody roads filled with the gloomy
ticking of time-clocks, time running down these roads
around hairpin turns, turning in on itself

during luminous moments
when love is found when love was sought
O Iridescent Keeper, of rainbowing laughter
              arching
music from a gold-capped grin

Of a bluesman, holding, the sun between
              his teeth

is where, you, miles, come from, playing roadhouse funk
funky soothsayer, of chewed-up moments played
clean, shekereman, at the crossroads of cardinal points
dropping dewdrop solos, of strut & slide
mean off into glide & stroll
talisman, hoodooing from bebop

trumpet voice walking on eggshells
mississippi river pouring from roots of your eyes

This poem appears in Weather Reports, a collection of
new and selected poems by Quincy Troupe, published
for Harlem River Press.

Appendix A

*Someday,
My Prince
(of Darkness?)
Will Come....
or
Miles of Love*

Miles's love life was a jazz composition marked by deep riffs, a touch of the blues, and the whole amalgam of emotions and apparent non sequiturs that is jazz.

Miles was married three times, and was the father of four. His first serious relationship was with a woman named **Irene Birth**, a slender woman with a dancer's body. In 1944, when she was nineteen and Miles was but sixteen, Irene gave birth to their first child, **Cheryl**. Two years later came their first son, **Gregory**; and then, in 1950, **Miles IV** was born. The relationship, however, was not a fulfilling one for either party, and was not to last. One problem was that they had been thrust together by the responsibilities of teen parenthood. Another problem was wanderlust. Wanderlust had Miles. And Miles's lust did wander.

MILESTIME...
MILES PROFESSED DEEP AND MEANINGFUL LOVE FOR PARTICULAR WOMEN OVER THE COURSE OF HIS LIFE, BUT THIS DID NOT PREVENT HIM FROM BEING INVOLVED WITH OTHER WOMEN AT THE SAME TIME. NOR DID IT IMPLY, SO FAR AS HE WAS CONCERNED, THAT HE DID NOT TRULY LOVE THE WOMAN TO WHOM HE DECLARED HIS LOVE AT ANY PARTICULAR TIME.

Upon meeting **Juliette Greco** in Paris in 1949, Miles discovered romantic love. Juliette aroused passions that no woman had before. All this without the aid of spoken language, as he didn't speak French, nor she English.

When Miles and Juliette parted after their initial two-week, whirlwind affair, Miles was cast into deep despair. And upon returning to the states Miles started whistling *Parker's Mood* due in part to longing for Juliette. This fact makes it easier for us to believe that he was truly moved by his time in gay Paree....

The years passed. Irene and the kids went back to St. Louis. Then, in 1953, on a trip to California, Miles met a beautiful, *"honey brown," "elegant, gracious, graceful"* woman named **Frances Taylor**. Frances, a dancer with, yes, a dancer's body, would become his first wife some seven years later.

In 1958, Frances re-entered Miles's life and things took off from there.. They married in 1960, and for a time lived a relatively normal domestic life. (Unfortunately Miles suffered from the Peter Peter Pumpkin Eater syndrome, and was inclined to that wife-in-a-pumpkin-shell thang.) In Frances, Miles found a happiness that he couldn't find in the street, nor from womanizing. Eventually, however, he got back into drugs and womanizing. In February of 1968, when his lifestyle became too much for her to bear, Frances left him. The sober Miles rued screwing this one up until the day he died

Later that year, the 42 year-old Miles married a gorgeous 23 year-old singer named **Betty Mabry**. Betty, his brown-skinned fountain of youth, introduced Miles to Jimi Hendrix and other black rockers who would greatly influence his music of that period. Aside from that, however, Betty didn't bring much to the table — at least not enough to sustain Miles, thus this marriage lasted only a year.

Early in '69 during his brief marriage with Betty, Miles became involved with **Marguerite Eskridge**, the mother of his fourth and last child, **Erin**. This four year relationship eventually ended because Marguerite couldn't accept Miles's wander-lust...

The lovely actress **Cicely Tyson** was Miles's third and last wife. They began their on-again, off-again relationship in 1968 and eventually got married on Thanksgiving, 1981. As Cicely and Miles got to know each other better, Miles felt they developed *"...this real tight spiritual thing."* Cicely had a very therapeutic effect on him as well. Like Frances, she was able to slow Miles down a bit, but this relationship seemed destined to fail, for Miles never really had a burning physical desire for Cicely. With Cicely Miles's shortcomings reached unparalleled lows. He struck other women, but he seemed to strike Cicely more. He cheated on other women, but he seemed to cheat on Cicely more...worst of all, he did so unabashedly.

MILESTIME:

IN HER BOOK, MAD AT MILES, *PEARL CLEAGE ASSERTS THAT* "MILES WAS GUILTY OF SELF-CONFESSED VIOLENT CRIMES AGAINST WOMEN SUCH THAT WE OUGHT TO BREAK HIS ALBUMS, BURN HIS TAPES AND SCRATCH HIS CD'S UNTIL HE ACKNOWLEDGES AND APOLOGIZES AND RETHINKS HIS POSITION ON THE WOMAN QUESTION."

Miles's relationship with his mother was, at times, very strained, especially during his teen years. Part of their conflict centered on Miles's brother Vernon. Vernon was homosexual, and Miles perceived Vernon's preference to be the result of his mother's emasculating pushiness. (Whether or not it was out of a need to prove his manhood in often brutal ways that led to what Cleage and others would characterize as Miles's misogynistic tendencies is, perhaps, best left to *Freud for Beginners* readers to discern.)

Miles had relationships and encounters too numerous to list. But, as Miles put it, he loved women. He loved to flirt. He loved to find out what made women tick. Some may doubt the validity of this assertion, but Miles felt that he truly had a lot of love to give. Perhaps it was just that his compassion too often played Rip Van Winkle — alive, but deeply immersed in sleep.

-Chris Long **123**

Miles Dewey Davis

Miles's odyssey spanned the world of modern jazz, winding its way from bebop to doo-bop. This *selecte* discography is your guide to that hip trek.

1940's
BIRD: THE COMPLETE CHARLIE PARKER ON VERVE (1946 -47) Verve
CHARLIE PARKER ON DIAL, VOLS. 4-6 (1947) EMI (Dial)
BIRD AT THE ROOST, VOL. 1 (1948) Savoy
IN PARIS FESTIVAL INTERNATIONAL DE JAZZ, (1949) CBS
BIRTH OF THE COOL (1949-50) Blue Note
1950's
MILES DAVIS AND HORNS (1951) PRESTIGE
CAPITOL JAZZMEN, METRONOME ALL STARS (1951) Capitol
MILES DAVIS VOL. 1 (1952-53) Blue Note
WALKIN' (1954) OJC
BAG'S GROOVE (1954) OJC
BLUE MOODS (1955) OJC
MILES DAVIS/MILT JACKSON ALL-STARS (1955) OJC
THE NEW MILES DAVIS QUINTET (1955) OJC
WORKIN' (1956) OJC
STEAMIN' (1956) OJC
RELAXIN' (1956) OJC
'ROUND ABOUT MIDNIGHT'(1956) Columbia
MILES AHEAD (1957) Columbia
ASCENSEUR POUR L'ECHAFAUD (1957) Phillips
MILESTONES (1958) Columbia
'58 SESSIONS (1958) Columbia
LEGRAND JAZZ (1958) Phillips
MILES AND MONK AT NEWPORT (1958) Columbia
PORGY AND BESS (1958) Columbia
KIND OF BLUE (1959) Columbia
1960's
SKETCHES OF SPAIN (1960) Columbia
STOCKHOLM (1960) Royal Jazz
SOMEDAY MY PRINCE WILL COME (1961) Columbia
LIVE AT THE BLACKHAWK Vol. 1 (1961) Columbia
LIVE AT THE BLACKHAWK Vol. 2 (1961) Columbia
AT CARNEGIE HALL (1961) Columbia
QUIET NIGHTS (1962) Columbia

Selected Discography

**The *ESSENTIAL RECORDINGS FOR BEGINNERS* are
bolded. These are some *terrible* sounds! Enjoy!**

SEVEN STEPS TO HEAVEN (1963) Columbia
MY FUNNY VALENTINE (1964) Columbia
'FOUR & MORE' (1964) Columbia
E.S.P. (1965) Columbia
MILES SMILES (1966) Columbia
SORCERER (1967) Columbia
NEFERTITI (1967) Columbia
WATER BABIES (1967-68) Columbia
MILES IN THE SKY (1968) Columbia
FILLES DE KILIMANJARO (1968) Columbia
IN A SILENT WAY (1969) Columbia
BITCHES BREW (1969) Columbia
CIRCLE IN THE ROUND (1955-70) Columbia
1970's
JACK JOHNSON (1970) Columbia
BLACK BEAUTY (LIVE AT FILMORE WEST) (1970) CBS-SONY
LIVE-EVIL (1970) Columbia
ON THE CORNER (1972) Columbia
BIG FUN (1969-72) Columbia
GET UP WITH IT (1970-74) Columbia
DARK MAGUS (1974) CBS-SONY
AGHARTA (1975) Columbia
PANGAEA (1975) Columbia
1980's
THE MAN WITH THE HORN (1980-81) Columbia
WE WANT MILES (1981) Columbia
STAR PEOPLE (1982-83) Columbia
DECOY (1983) Columbia
AURA (1984) Columbia
YOU'RE UNDER ARREST (1985) Columbia
FARENHEIT (1985) Columbia
TUTU (1986) Warner Bros.
SIESTA (1988) Warner Bros.
AMANDLA (1989) Warner Bros.
1990's
DINGO...CHIEN DU DESERT Warner Bros.
DOO-BOP (1992) Warner Bros.

Bibliography

Alkyer, Frank. *"The Miles Files."* New York: DOWN BEAT, December, 1991.

Birnbaum, Larry. *"Have They Delivered?"* Illinois: DOWN BEAT, JUNE 1992

Chambers, Jack. *MILESTONES: The Music and Times of Miles Davis.* New York: Quill William Morrow, 1983, 1985.

Cleage, Pearl. *Mad At Miles: A Blackwoman's Guide to Truth.* Michigan: The Cleage Group, 1990

Crow, Bill. *Jazz Anecdotes.* New York-Oxford: Oxford Un iversity Press, 1990.

Davis, Francis. *In The Moment: Jazz in the 1980's.* New York-Oxford: Oxford University Press, 1986.

Dennis, Denise. *Black History for Beginners.* New York: Writers and Readers Publishing, 1984.

Feather, Leonard. *The Encyclopedia of Jazz.* New York: Horizon Press, 1960

Godbolt, Jim. *The World of Jazz.* New Jersey: The Wellfleet Press, 1990.

Hentoff, Nat. *Jazz Is.* New York: Limelight Editions, 1991.

Lee, Jennifer. *"Last Miles."* New York: SPIN. December, 1991.

Low, W. Augustus. *Encyclopedia of Black America.* New York: Da Capo Press,

Lyons, Len. *Jazz Portraits: the lives and music of the jazz masters.* William Morrow 1989.

McRae, Barry. *Miles Davis.* London: Appollo Press Limited, 1988.

Rowland, Mark et. al. *"Sketches of Miles."* New York: MUSICIAN, December, 1991.

Troupe, Quincy. *Miles: The Autobiography.* New York: Simon & Schuster, 1989.

Troupe, Quincy. *Weather Reports.* Harlem River Press, 1991

⇥ᵀᵁᴸ◄ ⇥ᵀᵁᴸ◄ ⇥ᵀᵁᴸ◄ ⇥ᵀᵁᴸ◄ ⇥ᵀᵁᴸ◄ ⇥ᵀᵁᴸ◄ ⇥ᵀᵁᴸ◄ ⇥ᵀᵁᴸ◄ ⇥ᵀᵁᴸ◄ ⇥ᵀᵁᴸ◄

Photo/art credits

Acknowledgements

I'd like to thank **Pat Jones** for inviting me to Spike's book party and allowing me to deviate from my role as a *charming-but-vacuous boy toy on her arm to keep her drink refreshed* long enough to for me to meet Glenn Thompson; **Glenn Thompson** for his faith, patience, and commitment to the work that needs to be done; **Errol Selkirk** for helping to plant the idea.

Thanks to all those who sat in on my solo and helped me to improvise my way through this gig. **Michael de la Peña** for his friendship, support, and editing; **Mosh Süsser** & **Eric Velasquez** for their ears, hearts and hands; **Chris Long** , my brother, for words spoken, and even more important words never said; **Joy Allen and her Red Cowboy Boots** for that photoshop thang; **Deb "Debster" Dyson** for nudging me along; **Marie Brown,** my Queen, and the princesses: **Muki, Phyllis, Naadu; Kathy Bowser** and her trusty Mac; **Stephanie Richardson** and her Mac literate digits; **Rob Mills** for the IBM, and the *music;* **Tonya Williams** for helping to start the set; **Cynthia "I'm tooo fabulous" Walker** for keeping my eyes focused, (and **Wai,** too); **Jeff Mendelsohn** for that home stretch help; and **Beverly Peele** whose *Elle Magazine* spread adorned my work space and made the hours of work infinitely more bearable.

Thanks to *The Inner Circle Posse*: **Karen Long** (yo, sis, *thanks*), **Keith "Batman" Brown**, **Nathaniel Coleman, Neil de la Peña,** & **Jim Simpson**, jazz griot. *Y'all know what time it is.* And other comrades: **Liz Downing, Jasmine Alexander, Abby Schulhoff, Kevin Black, Jeanine Primm, Jeniffer Fell, Sungkey Paik, Ellene Hannah,** **Roger Bognar**.

Greetings to **Brian "Baby Bear" Williams** and his new wife. Bon Chance.

Thanks to **Quincy Troupe** for *"Four, and More."* To **Tracy Sherrod** for hookin' me up with Renee Foster. To the lovely **Renee Foster,** and to **Easy Mo Bee**. Here's to the *Doo-Bop.* Peace.

Last, I would like to extend *special* thanks to **Rosa "Baby Go-Go" Gomez** for the belief, for the madness, for the eyes. *Olacita.*

About the Author/Illustrator and contributing artists:

Daryl Long: *"I write, I draw, I hang out in cafes, all-day Kerouac-ing. I listen to jazz. Love jazz. Yes. I was a hell-raising teenager at New York's High School of Art and Design, stealing passes to the Museum of Modern Art and hanging out in front of Picassos after school with my comrades. Rowdy stuff like that. I'm better now, thanks. I live in Ft. Greene, Brooklyn. I attended Boston University. This is my first book. Thanks, Miles."*

Christopher Long: *" I hack around in Staten Island, NY due to the encouragement of Pamela K. Loor. The good doctor, GW McWilliams has been quite an inspiration as well, I must say. Carol AP Harris ...lunch? Uh, but no boots! Hey A. Christopher Black, JT Pendleton, the Long ones, Black ones, Norwich Free Academy and Trinity. Psi U!! Thanks, DNL!"* [Chris's writing appears on pages: 120-121.]

Moshe "MOSH" Süsser: *"I'm a cartoonist from Israel by way of Germany. It is difficult for me to say anything, I feel like a baby here in New York. I'm proud to be in this book, and to work with my brother Daryl. This kind of thing. Okay?"* [Mosh's drawings appear on pages: 6-7, 52-53 (a Daryl & Mosh collaboration of which we're very proud), 60-61, 112-113, 115.]

Eric Velasquez: *"Perfection! The word never meant much to me outside of the divine sense until I heard Miles play ' My Funny Valentine.' Then I knew what perfection was. Thank you, Miles."* [Eric's drawings appear on pages: 44, 78-79.]

Writers and Readers Documentary Comic Books
are excellent introductions to some of the major thinkers and
issues of our time. Comprising more than sixty titles, ranging
from *Architecture to Zen*, these fully illustrated *For Beginners*
books use wit, intelligence (and occasional irreverence), to bring
high ideas down to earth.

Started in England in 1974, the *For Beginners* books are avail-
able throughout the world, and are published in over fifteen
different languages.

For further information about the *For Beginners* series, please write

In the United States write to:

Writers and Readers Publishing
P.O. Box 461, Village Station
New York, New York
10014

In England & Europe write to:

Writers and Readers Publishing
c/o Airlift Book Company
26 Eden Grove
London N7 8EF England